"...if you believe, a lot of things follow from your belief."
Carl Sagan

"Imagination is more important than knowledge."
Albert Einstein

For in the unknown, there are possibilities that have no restrictions. When contemplating the unknown, your imagination has no limits.
Ralph Marston

Search is an excellent guide.
Rumi

"Two ways of thinking, the way of time and the way of eternity, are both part of man's effort to comprehend the world in which he lives. Neither is comprehended in the other, nor reducible to it, each supplementing the other, neither telling the whole story."
Robert Oppenheimer

I believe in the future resolution of two states (in appearance so contradictory), dream and reality, into a sort of absolute reality: Surrealite
Andre Breton

"You use the tools of science to understand how nature works, but you also recognize that there are things outside of nature, namely God, for which the tools of science are not well designed to derive truth."
Francis Collins, The National Human Genome Research Institute

My Neighbors' Ghosts

*For Antonia & Barney,
true believers!
Love, Katie*

MY NEIGHBORS' GHOSTS

KATIE LETCHER LYLE

MARINER PUBLISHING
BUENA VISTA, VIRGINIA

Copyright © Katie Letcher Lyle 2007

All Rights reserved, including the right of reproduction in whole or part in any form without the expressed written permission of the publisher.

Manufactured and Printed in the United States of America

1 3 5 7 9 10 8 6 4 2

Library of Congress Control Number: 2007900436
My Neighbors' Ghosts: and Other Amazing True Stories

p. cm.

1. Ghosts 2. Paranormal—Parapsychology 3. Synchronicity 4. Psychics
5. Spirituality—spiritualism, human transformation 6. Dreams
7. Near-death encounters 8. Psychophysical 9. Medicine and Psychology
10. Body and Mind Connection 11. Case Studies
I. Lyle, Katie Letcher   II. Title

ISBN-13: 978-0-9776841-5-1 (softcover : alk. paper)
ISBN-10: 0-9776841-5-6

Edited by Andrew Wolfe
Book & Cover design by Patricia Gibson

MARINER PUBLISHING
a division of
Mariner Companies, Inc.
212 East 21st Street
Buena Vista, VA 24416-2716
http://www.marinermedia.com

This book is printed on acid free paper meeting the requirements of the American Standard for Permanence of Paper for Printed Library Materials.

The Compass-Rose and Pen is a Trademark of Mariner Companies, Inc.

For my dear departed friend David McKnight,
whose skillful editing of this book in an earlier version
helped bring it to fruition,
for my dear departed Hospice patients,
and for my Monroe Institute friends,
and even for my unbelieving friends (Just have fun!):
from all of you I have learned
that I am more than my physical body.

I do not fear death because I know death is not the end.

Katie Letcher Lyle
April 2007

Contents

Introduction - Something After Death	13
1. My Neighbors' Ghosts	20
2. The Ghost of Anna Marie	53
3. The Greenbrier Ghost (1985)	56
4. Just Your Imagination?	69
5. Dreams	77
6. Chances of Chance: Synchronicities	90
7. Gifts from the Other Side: Apports	110
8. Angels	117
9. In and Out of the Body	122
10. Near Death Events	129
11. Poetic Justice, 1959	141
12. Across the Pond: British Stories	147
13. Objects with Minds of Their Own	152
14. Oddities	157
15. Predictions and Pitfalls	178
16. Conclusion: As Present As Possible	183
17. Further Reading for Spirit Chasers	189

INTRODUCTION

Something After Death

This is typical: The small white-haired lady, whose name I can't recall, leans forward over her grocery cart in Kroger and clutches her purse. She has heard I'm writing a book of ghost stories. The celery leaves tremble slightly as she tells her story.

"In 1918," she begins, "during the flu epidemic, my great-grandmother went to help out with her daughter, husband, and three children, all five of whom had the flu. It was summer, and she got off the train in the Oklahoma town where they lived, and hurried towards our house, which was then on the edge of town. Night was falling, and she heard beautiful singing voices ahead of her all the way to the house. Puzzled, she felt that the singers were just ahead of her and she'd catch up any minute. The gorgeous delicate voices with their perfect harmony gradually faded just as she reached the house; she never encountered the singers.

"Inside, all the house was in shock. The two youngest children had just died.

"Afterwards, they always believed that what my great-grandmother heard was the angels that had come for the children. My mother, the only surviving child, told me this."

What to make of such a story? As I continue my own shopping, I ponder how many of my friends and relatives would pooh-pooh it without question. Others would, of course, believe it entirely, perhaps on faith. Still others, made believers by experiences of their own, would chime in with their own "angel" or "amazing coincidence" or "ghost" stories. As a writer, a truth-seeker, all my life I have never known which position to take regarding tales that most would call *supernatural*. I've been asking people now for my whole life if they have any ghost stories.

Word is out around town that I'm collecting ghost stories for a book. Lexington is small, and most everyone knows most everything about most everybody.

I've been collecting and writing down stories for this book for over twenty years. But it's a subject so many find crazy, that I've been reluctant to even try to go public, to get it published. Even when I thought it might be finished, I've put it aside, and put it aside.

Finally, the editor of a publishing house in Rockbridge County asked to see the manuscript. Even then I was reluctant, and showed it to Andy Wolfe apologetically, saying I knew it wasn't ready.

In a very short time, he saw in the manuscript two books, one mostly the "ghost" stories I've heard from my friends and family and neighbors, though they are more accurately *stories that defy rational explanations*. The second book is more esoteric: he'd maybe like to title that one, *How to Talk to the Dead*.

My credentials for writing a book of this sort? Though I would never describe myself as psychic, I have had a lifelong interest in things paranormal. I have visited haunted houses when I could, sought out haunted sites in Europe and America, saved years of those predictions by psychics from magazines and newspapers, recorded particularly interesting dreams for about forty years, collected ghost stories from friends and strangers alike, and for a decade I was an active member of a ghost-hunting group. I own over a thousand, and have read at least twice that many, books about the paranormal. By profession, I'm a college English teacher; by avocation, I'm a writer.

I'm a hospice volunteer, and I occasionally practice my own form of healing touch (made entirely of *my intention to heal*) on my patients.

Since so-called *paranormal* events apparently absolutely do occur—there's little doubt about that—the error must be in the contemporary scientific paradigm. Believers in the so-called paranormal (though in widely-disparate polls, gathered who-knows-how? they represent from 30% to over 90% of us) are un-represented in government, business, or education. It was a national scandal when Nancy Reagan consulted a psychic, and Hillary Clinton was subjected to mocking headlines when she told of "communicating" with Eleanor Roosevelt. Nonetheless, there is, if you just go by numbers, overwhelming evidence that the dead still interact with the living. If even *some* of these stories are true, apparently part of what happens when we die is that we stay somehow connected with the living, perhaps through the vibration of mutual love—or sometimes hatred.

I conceived the idea for a book of "ghost stories" years ago, and began it as a hard skeptic in the seventies. I revisited the book a second time in the late eighties after writing a book entitled *The Greenbrier Ghost*. There's a chapter on that book. The trouble was, I could still explain away all paranormal events (including the ghost in that book)—though my interest in reading about those *woo-woo* subjects never flagged.

Not until I was over fifty did I find the spiritual path I needed to follow. This book will end with the beginning of my journey on that path. I want to leave it for the book that follows this one.

Despite the arch attitude of hard-line scientists, there has been in the past thirty years an explosion of confessional books by all sorts of otherwise-reasonable people who have experienced the sort of events I am writing about. Most are by ordinary people surprised by inexplicable events. Paranormal experiences are "out of the closet;" people from every class and culture report them.

All radical new *information* is at first ridiculed, then violently opposed, and finally, eventually, when the information turns out to be true, accepted as truth without fanfare. Although beliefs come into and out of fashion, we in our society are in the midstream of that ongoing process in regard to things currently dubbed "paranormal," but *which may be in fact perfectly normal*. A good example is that nearly everyone, even *doctors*, these days accepts the mind-body-spirit connection. That was not true as little as twenty or thirty years ago.

If you live in Rockbridge County, Virginia, you will recognize many of the people who appear in this book, and you will know, if you talk to them, that this book is not fiction.

Our house was on the local Garden Tour in April of 2002, for the third time in the nearly forty years we'd lived here. We were willing to open it to the hundreds of people who come annually to see Lexington houses: the proceeds from the Garden Week tour go to beautify our state and local highways, so I didn't mind the effort it took to wax, wash, polish brass, furniture, and copper, and repaint the most disreputable spots on walls and woodwork.

Several weeks before the tour, the garden club ladies needed to meet with me and talk about "traffic patterns" for the tour, the history of some of our furniture and paintings, in what spots their flower arrangements might most effectively be placed, where in our garden their members would be stationed, and what they would say to the visitors about the house. Offering the ladies coffee and tea, I chatted with them together and individually.

As we sat in the living room, one lady I didn't know well said brightly, "I hear your next book is about ghosts." Lexington is a small town, and I'm a known writer. I fend off questions all the time: *What's your next book about? What are you writing about?*

A slightly uncomfortable silence ensued. I said that was true, that I'd been tracking down paranormal stories in England and around these parts, but hadn't yet gotten the book organized. The party suddenly got awfully quiet.

Before another month had passed, I think that *every single one of the women* had made some excuse to call me—and to tell me of at least one anomalous, puzzling, or frankly paranormal experience in her own life. My impression was that they were reluctant to go public with the stories, since each one told me privately.

Obviously, a lot of people in the enlightened tiny city of Lexington, Virginia, in the first decade of the twenty-first century, still think it's a little peculiar, maybe embarrassing, or crazy, to believe in ghosts or angels, or out-of-body experiences—even if they themselves have experienced one of them. These women, at least some of them, were looking for answers, explanations, to unexplainable events in their lives. Others were quite matter-of-fact.

But the message I got, and indeed have gotten all my life, from friends and strangers alike, was, these things happen, and they can happen to anyone—even to members of the staid "Gyah-den Club of Virginia." "Tell my story," one said. "Yes, you can use my name." "Tell mine." "I've never told that to anyone, but you can tell it," said another.

And so I tell them here, theirs and my own. If you're a skeptic, raised in the fifties with the mid-twentieth century paradigms, there's *always* another explanation possible than the paranormal one. As I know well, you can rationalize any psychic event. Unfortunately, ghosts, intuitive flashes, amazing coincidences, and remarkable dreams aren't replicable or testable, the two demands of "scientific inquiry."

Yet, if nothing else, it seems reasonable to note that there are far too many ghost stories through the ages to suppose that all the experiencers are deluded or lying. And further, there are earthly proofs of information coming from beyond death.

It's exciting to me that some so-called paranormal claims have yielded of late to scientific inquiry: there is a solid and growing body of evidence that people can view places and events far distant from them in time and space; it's called "remote viewing." There is a growing amount of statistical evidence that prayer implements healing, whether the prayed-for know they are the subject of prayers or not; Larry Dossey is the authoritative voice on this subject. There is at least one impressive study of successful healing independent of place and time. It appeared in *Subtle Energies & Energy Medicine*, Vol. II, No. 3, pp. 207-239.

Here is what the researchers did: they chose at random patients in nursing care who had their vital signs measured daily. *Three months later*, volunteers each chose at random from those (randomly-chosen) patients *one* to pray for. When the researchers went back to the then *3-months old records*, the ones who had later been randomly selected and prayed for had *measurably better vital signs than the ones who had not been randomly chosen*.

For anyone willing to study the records of the past century of painstaking experiments, there is impressive evidence that psychic phenomena such as clairvoyance, precognition, mind over matter (psychokinesis), psychometry (gaining information from an object without knowledge of the object's provenance), and remote viewing (intent to allow part of your mind to go to some far location and describe it) are indeed real and true.

When I was a child, we listened to ghost stories at slumber parties, around campfires, but the subtle realms were not a proper subject for daytime conversation. The attitude has changed, in the almost seventy years I've been alive, from "Don't talk about such things. It's superstition and ignorance," to intelligent and sane people admitting to events that the scientific world denies. When I was a child, religion and spiritualism were opposites, almost as if religion was light and spiritualism dark. Today, it seems apparent that a belief in spirit, and in spirits, is coming into the mainstream.

Yet science, conventional, academic, and fearful of its precarious place at the apex of human knowledge, is slow to accept what the mainstream has perhaps never forgotten. Ann Druyan, widow of Carl Sagan, in an interview in *Discover* magazine (November 2003), spoke for the so-called rationalists, when she said, "...it's wrong to commit to a belief in the absence of evidence, especially when what you believe is transparently a palliative for your fear... You should not believe anything for which there is no [scientific] evidence." Druyan has shut her eyes firmly to any possibility of any paranormal event. She is the way I was before I began to notice.

1

My Neighbors' Ghosts

I've found that you only have to scratch lightly to uncover anomalous experiences in most peoples' lives. Try it: ask anyone, "Have you ever seen a ghost?" Oh, many folks when asked may at first say *No, I don't believe in ghosts. But then*, they go on, their gaze growing dreamy: *...there was this one strange thing that happened...* and they are off, telling you some "paranormal" yarn.

Probably more than half the population of our ill-defined area known as Appalachia would agree that something of us survives earthly death, and that, on occasion, that something interacts with the living—whether they themselves have seen a ghost or not.

Curiously, in St. Cloud, Minnesota, in the nineteen-seventies a Reverend Ben Johnson with a Harvard doctorate did an extensive survey of "strange experiences that don't square with assumed reality." His conclusion, in that city of 45,000 people, was that 30% of the population reported religious visions, prophetic dreams, heavenly voices, or ghostly visitations. Although St. Cloud seems far from the Valley of Virginia, I suggest that what he found is about typical for America in general.

Most, if not all, primitive cultures believe the dead can be contacted from the world of the living. I've studied enough to be able to say that many (I can't say all, because I don't know that) American native peoples considered it a perfectly reasonable act to go communicate with a dead ancestor on a nearby mountaintop or sacred spot—to help solve this life's problems.

On National Public Radio's "All Things Considered," in March 2003, a West Virginia woman reported that she had gone to the nearby cemetery and prayed to her dead grandfather to help her to stop the destructive mountaintop coal mining that persists in that state, and was encroaching on her home. A day later in the library she stumbled upon an old law that prevented mountaintop coal mining within a certain number of feet of a cemetery—and saved at least one mountaintop from being stripped, leveled off, and mined. *She stated that she believed her dead grandfather led her to that law.*

Here are a few of my friends' and relatives' and my own ghost stories. First, a word about the ghosts themselves: Celia Green, in her book *Apparitions*, remarks that ghosts of people known to the perceiver usually come in three forms: they look as they did at the time of their death; or they appear to be at the prime of life, generally in their mid-thirties; or they look nothing like they did in life *though the perceiver knows clearly who the person is*. I have picked up examples of all three.

As word of this project got around town, I heard tale after tale of ghosts that appear at the ends of beds, of chairs that rock without visible agency. I heard a story about the ghost of a woman I knew when she was alive haunting the house she lived in; she was a scary presence alive, and I imagine would be a scary presence dead. I heard of objects that disappear then mysteriously reappear months or even years later. I heard of a house built on what was once a railroad right-of-way: it rumbles sometimes, and the folks living there occasionally hear the sound of a train going by. I heard of two ghost cats and a ghost dog. I heard of a man who died coughing 2000 miles away from his daughter; she, telling me the story, wept, explaining how she woke up from a deep sleep, distinctly hearing her father cough. Her pets, a cat and a dog, she noticed also reacting to the coughing just as if someone were in the house. She called the hospital where she knew her father to be, and confirmed that he had indeed just died—coughing.

I have captured in photographs what the eye cannot see. No one, as far as I know, has been able to explain away certain light blobs or "orbs" in photos of supposedly empty rooms in haunted houses. One opinion is that they are spirits, undetectable to the human eye but detectable by digital camera.

I have some friends who appear frequently throughout this book. Two of them are Mary and David McKnight. They lived, in the years I knew them, near McDowell, in rural western Virginia. I met them in 1992 while taking a course taught by David, a Harvard graduate and retired Presbyterian minister, through Discovery University, the brilliant brainchild of another friend, Wendy Bush Hackney. One could take mini-courses at most reasonable rates in herblore, plant identification, folk medicine, and many other things, including *ghost-hunting*. I took several of those courses, all excellent—and taught one called "intuitive cooking." So I signed up for David's course, and we became friends immediately. For ten years afterwards we had an informal ghost-busting group; we would visit haunted houses by invitation of people who heard about us, and try to contact the haunting spirits to send them on to higher levels. David was a minister with a degree from Union Theological Seminary, a college professor, a lecturer on thanatology, the afterlife, ghost-hunting. His wife Mary is a psychic, a channeler, a writer and an artist. She is highly intuitive. David has now died, and Mary lives in Canada, but we communicate frequently.

Once at the McKnight's house, shortly after Mary's mother had died, I took two pictures of my daughter Jennie Lyle and Mary McKnight cutting up vegetables for supper. A moment after I took the first snapshot, Mary remarked quietly, "Oh, I think my mother has come." As I was still standing holding my new digital camera, I snapped a second picture instantly. We could see the pictures immediately. On the first, there is nothing. On the second, above Mary's head, taken maybe six or eight seconds after the first photo, is a bright glowing orb. Is it the ghost of Mary's mother?

Many people ask if I am planning to retell Rockbridge County's most famous nineteenth century ghost story, about a poltergeist called the McChesney Ghost. It's the story of a fearful supernatural siege by a poltergeist (a ghost who throws things, literally) against a prominent and wealthy family living in the northern part of the county. Horrifying events were witnessed and testified to in 1825 by some of Rockbridge County's most upstanding physicians, men of God, lawyers, even a college president. A young Caribbean slave girl owned by the McChesney family first claimed to be tormented by invisible pinches and pricks, but soon the whole family experienced falling stones indoors and outdoors, clods of dirt flying about the house and injuring people, loud obscene noises, and heavy furniture piled mysteriously in the middle of rooms. A neighbor was severely injured by a flying rock, and Dr. McChesney was bombarded by earthen lumps when he challenged the spirit to "come out and fight like a man."

Not until the slave (Maria) was sold did the disturbances stop. Unfortunately, there are no accounts of what happened at the next place Maria went to stay.

I say, "No, I don't think I'll repeat that over-told story."

There are stories by two people who still live in the McChesney house: both told local reporters recently that the house is still "haunted" by footsteps, objects that move without human intervention, creaks, voices. However, their stories were not specific enough to repeat here.

Dr. Richard Moore, a physician who practiced for a few years in Lexington, grew up at the edge of Hollywood Cemetery in Richmond. He told me that he and a friend, when they were about eight, once watched a young adult couple in exquisite nineteenth century clothing taking a leisurely walk through the cemetery—only their feet seemed to be about a foot off the ground.

My neighbor Taylor Sanders, a Washington and Lee history professor, and I often chat about local history. We struck up a conversation one day while he was walking his dog Marco Polo. I told him I was collecting stories for this book and he promptly told me he grew up in a house haunted by the protective ghost of a magician in a red smoking jacket whom they thought was named Max, whom Taylor often saw out of the corner of his eye. (Taylor's own father was a living magician, a colleague and friend of the famous Thurston and Blackstone.) There are many stories, but this one is the best.

Once when he was a teenager, Taylor reported, a boyfriend of his sister's stood embracing her at the bottom of the stairs on a night when their parents were not home. Over her shoulder the young man suddenly gasped, drew back, and stammered that he had to leave. Taylor's sister, puzzled, asked what was wrong. "Your father's *not* out; he's up there watching us," the boy replied.

"But my parents are *both* out, they've gone out of town," Taylor's sister insisted. The boy then asked, "Then who's the guy in the red coat?" He left hastily, and only later did the teenagers realize that Max had apparently appeared to scare off the sister's beau. The temptation of an empty house might have led to dangerous activity.

Recently my dear friend and fellow writer Janet Lembke who describes herself as a skeptic, told me in the most matter-of-fact way that her neighbor, whose Staunton kitchen window is only yards from hers, has told her that in the months since her husband's death, he, the neighbor, has twice seen "the Chief" (her husband) standing over Janet as she worked in her kitchen on her computer, though Janet herself says she has not felt his presence.

Pat Fitzberger Gibson was a student of mine at Southern Seminary College, where I taught from 1962-1987. Pat's life took several turns she never expected. While living and working in Germany, she and her husband separated. She and her two children moved to her home state of Maryland, to Annapolis, where her parents lived. As much as they loved being near the water and her parents, it was obvious that this was not the place where they were supposed to be. Her son did not fit in well in his new school. In fact the headmistress informed Pat that her son wouldn't be allowed back the next year. Not knowing what to do, or where to go, she got in her car and found herself in Buena Vista. Seeking the counsel of Thelma Lomax, the alumnae director at Sem and a dear friend, Pat said she was willing to do anything to find the right home for her and the children. Thelma told her that she needed to move to BV, that everything would be just fine.

Leaving Thelma's office, Pat drove down one of the streets that leads from the campus. In just a few blocks, she found an old house, much in need of repair, with a For Sale sign out front and a big magnolia tree in the yard. It seemed to be calling out to her, and right then and there she knew that was The House. She bought it, in as-is condition in February 1988. Even without heat the empty old house seemed "warm and rosy." From the beginning she'd felt this "open," pleasant, benign male presence in the house. In the months before she could move back, she got calls from the police about finding open doors and windows nearly every day. She put in deadbolt and chain locks, asked the police to maintain surveillance, but nothing seemed able to keep a door, a window, from being open each time the officers checked the house. The house was rumored to be haunted, and this seemed to reinforce local opinion. But that wasn't the only thing ...

Once her soon-to-be ex-husband visited, and laid his Ray-Ban sunglasses down somewhere in the empty house. They vanished, and have never reappeared. (Perhaps the ghost wanted to "unmask" him.) He also owned a set of keys to her parents' house, which also vanished while he was in her house. Pat was relieved he could no longer let himself in to her parents' house, but her mother was furious. She accused him of hiding the keys out of spite. The keys were returned to Pat about a year later, just appearing one day on a sideboard she had just finished polishing.

One day as she and the children sat at the dining room table discussing what color to paint the house, drinking apple juice, she mentioned mauve—and the apple juice pitcher tipped over, spilling the remaining juice. No one was near it. Puzzled, Pat cleaned it up, and they went back to the discussion with a new pitcher of juice. "I like mauve," she said, having remembered a beautiful mauve Victorian house in Annapolis that she had always liked. The second pitcher of juice overturned at that moment. She painted the house yellow.

Pat read in an issue of *Old House Journal* that if you felt you had a ghost, you should communicate with your spirit. She made sure the children weren't around—and neither was anyone else. She spoke to "whomever" one day close to Halloween, telling him he was welcome to stay there, that she loved the house and wanted to bring it back to life. She also asked that he not frighten her children, and that he not appear to her face to face.

She decided to mention her "ghost" to her next-door neighbor Bill Dickinson, who tended to the twin magnolia trees in their yards. At once he said, "Oh, I know who that is; that's my Uncle Will, who lived there. If it's anybody, that's who it has to be! He just loved that house."

So Uncle Will became the spirit of the house and the patron saint of lost objects. He always deposited them in plain view, sometimes right in the middle of the floor, but always, nowhere near where they could have been, and often in places that had already been searched. Pat felt his presence often, feeling he was a spirit, not a ghost.

Bill suddenly died near Labor Day, before he could tend his beloved trees. He wanted branches from his magnolia and, Pat says, both magnolia trees bloomed, allowing his coffin to be topped with magnolia blossoms, as he had wished. (The famous botanist M.L. Fernald writes that magnolias bloom usually in May or June, —but also sometimes into the autumn.) Uncle Will is still with Pat and seems to thoroughly approve of her *new* husband Keith. They were married in the house—and they are *sure* they had one unseen guest at the wedding.

I have another story of a botanical—or perhaps entomological—oddity; one day in summer Mickey Watkins, our volunteer coordinator at Rockbridge Area Hospice, was called to pronounce the death of one of our patients. There was a small tree just outside the door of the little house. When she went into the house, the tree was green. She signed the death certificate, visited a bit with the family, and left.

The sun was going down, and suddenly she noticed that the tree was now white. She stopped to stare, and saw that the little tree was covered with tiny white butterflies, all trembling together, making the tree appear white. She went back into the house and told the family, and all of them stood amazed, watching the white tree seeming to breathe as one entity. It seemed to Mickey, who frankly admits not understanding the phenomenon, that nature was acknowledging the passing of a gentle spirit.

For over fifty years I have kept notebooks and files on anomalous events in ordinary people's lives. As I began to pull this book together from piles and piles of stuff I'd filed, it gained momentum of its own.

For instance, when I casually mentioned to my friend and cross-street neighbor Georgianna Brush, godmother of my daughter, and one of Lexington's most prominent artists, that I was writing a book about paranormal events, she immediately leaned over her garden gate and told me this story:

"Once my mother woke suddenly at 2:00 a.m. envisioning flames and knowing something was wrong with one of her children. It was while my brother was at Kenyon College. Next morning she learned that his dorm had burnt down at the exact time she had awakened. He had barely gotten out alive."

And later that same day I had lunch with David and Mary McKnight, when David told me this story:

"Once my grandmother went to her bedroom to get a fur piece to wear out to dinner. She had laid it out on the bed; but she did not turn on the light when she went into the room. As she bent to pick it up, something grabbed her shoulders and pulled her back. At the same moment she heard a sharp, *No!*

"Startled by this, my grandmother returned to the room where my grandfather was and described what had just happened. Was there an intruder? Together they returned to the bedroom and, switching on the light, saw a poisonous scorpion on the fur piece. Who or what warned her of the danger?"

Mary McKnight chimed in with a story: "Once in the sixties, my brother was driving a Volkswagen, and stopped for a stoplight. When the light changed, and he pressed his foot on the accelerator, nothing happened. As he with some annoyance pressed the accelerator again, a truck hurtled by just in front of him, having run the red light. It would have hit him had his car responded when he first tried to accelerate. After the truck went by, the accelerator worked fine. He believes he was saved by some protective force."

In one of my Elderhostel classes at the Natural Bridge Hotel, a woman came up privately to tell me an experience. She had driven, as usual, to pick up one of her children after school. While waiting at a stoplight, she was suddenly overcome with an unfamiliar stark, cold terror. She broke out in a sweat, felt dizzy, feared she would vomit or faint, and had to turn around and drive home. She recalled that *she could not understand why all the other people waiting for the light to change looked perfectly normal, not upset at all.*

She weakly made her way home, arranged for someone else to pick up her child, and sat down with a cup of tea trying to recover from the severe sick panic she had felt. She was also puzzled at her peculiar symptoms.

That night, the six o'clock newscast was interrupted to announce that the dismembered body of a missing twelve-year-old boy had been found in a dumpster that was only *feet* away from where she had been waiting for the light to change when the feeling of terror hit her. She believes that she clairvoyantly experienced vibrations from that event, or mental telepathy from the victim's spirit, as nothing remotely like that has happened any other time in her life.

My mushroom-hunting buddy of forty years, Burwell Wingfield, is a biology professor at Virginia Military Institute in Lexington. He saw his mother in their house several times after her death, looking just as she had in life. On the night he mentioned it to the rest of his family, it turned out that one of his sons, and his wife, now-ex, had seen her too.

Sally Drake Sessoms, whom I have known all my life, is quite psychic. I'm looking for the right color paint for something I'm wanting to repaint. She's standing at the front counter of the store where she works, Rockbridge Interiors, telling me casually how she woke up one morning when she was in college, and told her roommate that she had dreamed that a mutual friend of theirs had been killed in a car accident. At breakfast, the dean interrupted the meal to announce the death of the student Sally had dreamed of. Sally says her roommate stared at her, and said, "You must have been listening in on the phone." But Sally had been sound asleep.

So Sally accepts ghostly activities as a normal part of life. She lived for many years in a house just around the corner from mine, built in the last decade of the nineteenth century. She says the strong scent of perfume would appear out of nowhere, and vanish just as quickly. Chairs rocked by themselves in that house. Once when her future son-in-law, a man definitely not given to fantasy, she emphasizes, was at the dining room table studying for an exam, he suddenly felt a swift, definite and threatening presence walk by him behind his chair, and the hair on the back of his neck stood straight up. There was no one there. In the house things would disappear, be gone for up to a year, and reappear. Some items that disappeared never reappeared.

And when Sally's vibrant mother, Virginia Drake, died, her children and grandchildren were cooking at her house for a gathering after the funeral, discussing some controversial subject. Suddenly six people in Sally's kitchen all saw a heavy frying pan jump from a back burner to the floor of the kitchen, with no one anywhere nearby. The family laughed, sure that Virginia Drake was still making her strong opinions known from the other side.

Lindsey Weilbacher, a newspaper reporter now gone from the area, lived in the sixties in an 1826 house near Fairfield that she believed was haunted by the spirit of an Indian, apparently a chief—though she emphasized that she herself did not believe in ghosts. She pointed out to me a cold area on the landing of the stairs that just about everyone noticed. (I imagined that I felt cold there too, but attributed the sensation to my imagination.)

Here's the story: her husband Ed fell down the steps from the landing three times, claiming he had been tripped each time. Then one night while they watched TV, Ed stared out into the hall where the steps were and said, "Oh, my God. Do you see him?"

"What?" she asked. When he could talk again, Ed described a tall man he had seen standing with his hand on the newel post, seeming to stare into the room at them. The figure was long-haired, with no face that Ed could see, wearing a long cloak or fluffy robe of some sort. Several days later, Ed found a perfect arrowhead in the dirt directly under the stairs, a spot he'd crawled in many times before.

He and Lindsey decided not to mention anything about Ed's perception to their eight-year-old daughter, Dorothy. They continued to find and collect many arrowheads on the property, but never mentioned Ed's experience to Dorothy, whose room was directly over the spot where Ed had seen the figure. Then one night she moved out of her bed to a sofa in her room to allow a visiting great-aunt to sleep in her bed. After the aunt left, Dorothy flat out refused to sleep in her room by herself. When her parents cajoled the truth out of the little girl, Dorothy told them she'd awakened to find a tall figure standing by her bed and staring down at her sleeping aunt. She was sure it was a "he" and described to them a six-foot-tall figure wearing "something funny like a robe with feathers on it." It did not go away. She could see no face, but the figure appeared intent on her great-aunt. When she could stand it no longer, she slipped off the couch and ran out of the room quickly.

Neither father nor daughter saw the figure again. Dorothy slept in another room from then on. At some point, they invited an archaeologist to view their arrowheads, and he dated them to 6500 years ago. As the house is built near a vigorous spring, the archaeologist opined that this could have been a watering spot for native people all those many years ago, and a tool-making area.

When years later I visited the Weilbacher house, I asked the new owner, Frank Harralson, if he'd heard that story. Seeming surprised, Frank instead told me about finding a perfect arrowhead in the basement, on the now-concrete floor, directly underneath the "cold spot" Lindsey had shown me. He had not heard any story about an Indian nor seen one. The Harralsons believe the house to be haunted by the spirit of a young girl from the early twentieth century who drowned in their pond, and appears to be delicate, maybe seven or eight, as well as by a cat ghost that all of the family members have caught glimpses of.

Hale Broce, a friend and fellow-writer from Covington, relates that his aunt Arlene was devastated when her beloved husband Pickett died. No one could coax her out of her depression. She was only 65, but she wanted to die too. Then, she told Hale, one night about a year after Pickett's death, something jerked her awake, and she knew there was someone in the room with her. Terrified, Arlene peered into the darkness. As her eyes adjusted, there at the foot of her bed stood her husband. Gently he told her he was happy, that he was well, and that he wanted her to stop grieving and to go on with her life. After that, although she wasn't sure if she'd had a dream or a real visit, Arlene's depression lifted. She told Hale that the visit gave her the greatest relief, and afterwards she felt entirely at peace. She has continued to get better ever since.

Bradley Harold Barber is neither a believer nor a disbeliever. He'd never had anything odd happen to him—except for a few dreams. He worked alone a lot in Andy Wolfe's house one summer, mostly painting trim, some of which took six coats. It was summer, the upstairs of the slate-roofed house sometimes reaching 115 degrees after noon. He noted a lot of funny feelings, and often had what he calls a cold chill. At the same time, his nephew worked across the county at Sunnyside, a venerable house being restored.

It was reputed to be so haunted that one workman walked off the job and left his tools, and wouldn't go back in the house for them. Bradley felt chills, odd feelings of being watched, and every so often, he would turn and get a glimpse of a shimmering light, sort of like a very sheer curtain blowing. He'd work upstairs in the mornings until it got too hot, then move downstairs.

Late one day he was working downstairs in the kitchen. The back door was open. Over his right shoulder he caught a glimpse of something sparkly; it seemed, he says, like antron, a nylon fishing line material that trout fishermen use, that flashes in sunlight. He turned and saw a form, like a sheer curtain, which he immediately identified as female, though it had no shape. It floated down the 50 foot long hall that led to the front door, and vanished, in no more time than a "grouse flush," that heart-stopping moment that a grouse explodes from the underbrush in front of you. Two or three heartbeats, he thinks. He says he was not scared, just startled. "You know what you've seen," he finishes, "and the good Lord knows what you have seen."

He never mentioned it to anyone until the day Andy began to talk about "the spirit in the house." Andy thinks the spirit is a female named Robbie, who once lived in the house. Andy and his family have a cordial relationship with Robbie. According to local folklore, on the last day of her life, Robbie made an appointment to have her hair done, dressed for the appointment, got her hair washed and set, came home, lay down, and died. Andy feels her friendly presence often, and feels he knows what room she prefers, even her favorite color (red), and so has in his living room a red chair for Robbie.

At that point Bradley told Andy what he'd seen. A final note: Bradley was playing the New Testament on his tape recorder the day he saw Robbie, or whoever she is.

Friend and writer Charlotte Morgan, headmistress of a small school, saw a ghost once when awaking from her bed in a college dorm. A woman's form appeared right in front of her, saying nothing but seeming like a protective spirit. It was no one she knew, no message she could detect. Charlotte felt it might have been someone who'd been dorm-mother in the past. Her roommate never woke up, and the ghost never returned for a second visit.

Monty Leitch, *nee* Monty Simmons, a writer for the *Roanoke Times*, has seen two ghosts. One day when she was in high school she passed a house reputed to be haunted, and saw a "liquid whiteness" moving behind a broken window. Her mother convinced her she'd seen nothing but the wind moving a curtain or rocking a chair.

Today she lives in an old house, and she woke one night when the moon was full to see a woman in a wicker chair in her bedroom, a "pale, wavering, blue" gazing out the window. Monty blinked, and the lady vanished. Monty's watched the chair ever since when the moon is bright, but has never seen another figure like the one she saw that once.

My ex-husband's cousin Anne Patterson Braly and I have become close. She is the Food Editor of the *Chattanooga Times Free Press*. She told me that while she was attending her grandfather's funeral at Masannetta Springs, Virginia, she was asleep in a dorm-like room provided by the retirement center with some other family members who had traveled long distances for the event, when she was sharply awakened by first a rustling, then a whooshing sound. She opened her eyes, and there was a face right in front of her, and a voice that didn't come from the lips but did come from the apparition, asking simply, "Are you okay?" Then the face receded, seeming to swiftly back up, and vanished.

Next morning, Anne ascertained that none of the other relatives there for the funeral had seen anything. The figure was not one she recognized. He was male, young, dark-haired—she estimates mid-thirties—and seemed to her a little like her grandfather Sam Houston (collateral descendant of the famous one) might have looked when young. Of course she had not known her grandfather at that age. Anne's conclusion is unequivocal: "People who do not believe in the Afterlife are just stupid!"

Al Watkins, a licensed social worker for Rockbridge Area Hospice, knew his mother was sick, but believed she was going home the next day from the hospital. In the night, he felt a hand brush his face, waking him up. As he stirred, his wife Mickey beside him woke, and he mumbled, "That was Mother."

"What was?" Mickey asked, confused.

"I don't know why I said that," Al admitted sleepily. "I felt a hand. I thought it was Mother."

In that instant, the phone rang. It was Al's brother calling from the hospital to tell him that their mother had just died unexpectedly.

Friends Merrie Gayle and John McNemar bought a pre-Civil War house in Lexington that had stood empty for 35 years before they began their restoration of it. Merrie Gayle owns Rockbridge Interiors in Lexington, and John is a consulting engineer. In researching the house, they learned that the builder, the original owner of the house, had later lost a leg in the Civil War, and eventually had died in a prison camp in Pennsylvania.

There was much work to be done to the house. The painters and carpenters, and the family members, were edgy about the fact that doors opened and closed by themselves, and that sometimes a room would get as cold as the inside of a refrigerator.

One day Merrie Gayle and her two sons and some of their friends were in the kitchen, knocking out a divider with sledgehammers, when her youngest, Andrew, said, "Hey, Mom, look at the doorknob.

It's going round and round all by itself." The older boys took a look, dropped their hammers, and ran.

There was no electricity in the house during the time they were working, and one cold night Merrie Gayle sent her oldest son and a pal upstairs with flashlights to close some windows that had been left open to air the room out. The boys soon came running down, both insisting that they had done as she asked—but that as soon as their backs were turned, both windows flew open again.

The house had two heavy sets of front doors, one solid wood, the other walnut and glass, and once while the family all were sitting in the den, both sets of doors flew open forcibly, though there was no wind.

Friends staying in the downstairs guest room were kept awake deep in the night by a thump thump thump sound, like that of a cane striking the stair treads, perhaps the sound of a one-legged man descending. After John and Merrie Gayle carpeted the stairs, that sound never recurred.

Merrie Gayle feels from the evidence that the builder of the house, the one-legged Civil War veteran, is certainly the haunter. During a deep snow in 1993, they happened to look out a second story window, and there was one perfect bootprint in the snow on the porch roof. When they went around looking, there was one more out another window, both single prints too far out for someone to have reached a boot and stamped a print as a joke. There were no footprints or other marks in the new blanket of snow that anyone planting such a thing could have left. The family and workmen were startled, but not really afraid—when more than one person was there. But no one wanted to be alone in the house.

Merrie Gayle, who is Catholic, said loudly one day when she was in the house alone, "Look, I don't mind your being here. But you must stop scaring us. Don't mess with us. We are trying to fix up your house and my family wants to live here, and you're scaring everyone." After that, she says, they were not bothered.

But one final event assures her the ghost is still there, perhaps mollified now that he has been acknowledged. All four of the front doors warped after a time, and stuck, and needed to be shaved down. And so one Saturday afternoon John took one of the outer walnut doors, which weighed around two hundred pounds, off the hinges and laid it down to work on it. Merrie Gayle went off to Mass. John is the rational one, the non-believer.

While she was gone, the wind began to blow, and John decided he'd better replace the door on its hinges to prevent drafts, but found the weight of the door too much for him. When Merrie Gayle returned from Mass, she said John was white as a sheet. He told her he'd tried and tried to boost the door up on the hinges, and just could not lift it up by himself, when suddenly the door just lifted and slipped over the hinges *for all the world as if someone else had helped him lift it.*

In 1967, Evan Jeffries, a Washington and Lee University student, told me of living over a store that is catty-cornered from the Lexington Post Office, and awakening one night to find a man leaning over him: tall, slender, balding, in a hard-brimmed straw hat worn on the back of his head. The man was bent, with a long face. As Evan watched, he appeared to turn and descend as if down stairs, though there were no stairs where he walked. He disappeared eventually through the floor. Taking this event seriously, Evan later ascertained that the staircase in the house had formerly been exactly where he saw the fellow descend. Efforts to discover the identity of the man failed, despite his specific description.

A young friend of mine, Brevin Balfry, while in high school had a job as a waiter at a local restaurant called the Willson-Walker House. One night late he was sent upstairs to a storeroom for something. As he passed a hallway leading to the upstairs rest rooms, he caught sight of a figure that shocked and scared him: a tall, thin man in old-fashioned evening clothes and a top hat stood in the hallway, peering malevolently out at him. Already past the hallway, Brevin backtracked, took another look to see who it might be up there where no patrons were supposed to be, but the hall appeared empty. Brevin managed to never again venture up to the second floor.

Barbara Wassell Goldsten of Lexington is a recent friend. Her first husband was in the Navy, and they moved to New Jersey when he retired. After her husband died of lung cancer in 1992, Barbara moved to Rockbridge County from New Jersey to be near her daughter, Elizabeth Wassell Sauder, an artist married to local blacksmith Lee Sauder. In 1998 she married widower Joe Goldsten.

When Barbara first moved to Rockbridge County she redid an old country cabin, connecting it to the nearby smokehouse with a gallery-library. Her bedroom was the smokehouse, which had two big windows. The curtains were usually open, for she liked moonlight flooding in, and in the country there was no reason to close them.

One night she awakened in terror, for a man with red hair and odd clothing was coming in her door from the library. As any of us might under the circumstances, she pretended to be asleep, sure that at any moment he was going to rape her. He walked carefully around to the unused side of the bed, at her back, and she felt his weight on the bed, felt him get in bed beside her. In terror she waited.

He did nothing. After an interminable wait, she feigned waking up, and with her foot reached behind her, where she felt his foot. He didn't move. Still frightened, she slowly turned over in bed, and looked at him. He was lying apparently asleep. She remembers his slightly out-of-date loose white shirt and baggy tannish pants, not modern clothes but not outlandishly old-fashioned either. Finally, she reached out and felt him. He felt real. Then instantly he vanished.

Shocked, she saw that he was no longer there, reached for her lamp switch, and turned on the light. There was nobody in the room with her. She checked the entire house, which was locked up tightly anyway, but there was nobody. He never returned.

My now-deceased friend Lee Kahn woke one night in the house he and his family had just moved into in Lexington, to find a lady peering down at him. He told me he waked his wife Betty to see this woman, but Betty saw nothing. He described the woman in minute detail, and they began to check with neighbors. Neighbors told them that his description fit Mrs. McClure, a previous owner, the widow of a dentist, who had inhabited their house until her death. However, there'd been interim owners, and the Kahns had never known Mrs. McClure.

When Jo Anne Mantz's strong-minded grandma died, the chair in which the old woman had habitually sat in the kitchen was put up in the attic, to afford more room. Immediately the family were treated to a panoply of footsteps, chair rocking, doors opening, and they could actually follow the sounds of footsteps downstairs and into the kitchen.

It was the children who heard, while their mother, who worked away from home, kept telling them it was just their imaginations, and to quit being so dramatic—until finally one day Jo Anne's mother heard one of the manifestations, and was absolutely terrified. The children all "knew" by then that it had to do with Grandmother's chair. Once they got their mother's attention, she threw out the chair, and no one ever heard sounds again.

Jessica Simanek, now of Mount Pleasant, South Carolina, knew a little boy who was a friend of her daughter. The boy kept telling his mother about a friend named Eejie. The child's mother knew the neighborhood kids, and had never met Eejie, so she asked her little boy which one of the neighborhood children Eejie was.

The child replied, "He's the one with the hole in his head. He lives up on the street behind us."

Still puzzled, the mother asked the other neighbors, including Jessica, if they knew Eejie, but none of the other mothers or any of their children did. But her child kept talking about what Eejie said, what Eejie did.

The mother had her child take her around to show her which was Eejie's house. But the people living there knew of no Eejie, though the child insisted that Eejie did too live there.

The story finally began to make sense when another neighbor on the street remembered that a previous owner, a Mr. E.G. Tatum, had committed suicide by shooting himself in the head.

Ann Carrington Tutwiler Rogers, now Ann Carman, is a lifelong friend of mine. We were childhood friends, went to Hollins College together, then had a thirty-year gap while she lived abroad and elsewhere with her missionary husband. They returned to Lexington, he taught at Washington and Lee for a few years, and then died. After his death we took to walking together several miles several times a week, and became even closer than we had been as children. She became a professor of Japanese at Washington and Lee, was an avid reader, a skeptic, and one of the most endearing friends I have ever had. My lifelong nickname for her is "Tut," and she appears in several stories in this book.

Tut's relationship with her mother was somewhat distant and formal. While everyone in the family knew her mother was dying of cancer, no one talked about it, and Mrs. Tutwiler died with many things unspoken, stoical and upbeat to the end, gracefully covering up her lack of appetite, saying such things as, "Oh, thanks, I'll eat that later…"

The night after Mrs. Tutwiler died, Tut dreamed of her mother looking lovely, young, and healthy. In the dream, Tut exclaimed, "Mother! What are you doing here? I thought you were dead!"

Her mother replied, "Why, of course I'm not. Whoever in the world told you that?" Virtually the same dream has occurred to two more of my friends: their mothers, a confrontation, the mother each time denying being dead.

My own mother appeared in a dream to her sister, my Aunt Polly. My mother said to her, accusingly, "What are you doing in my blue sweater?" Aunt Polly had asked my father for the sweater after Mama died. Polly now laughs at how, when they were girls, she used to sneak-borrow her older sister's clothes and not take care of them, whereas Betty (my mother) was always careful and precise about her clothing.

Polly replied, "Well, I thought it was okay to take it, since you're dead."

"How ridiculous!" my mother said. "I certainly am *not* dead!" Though my mother died in 1979, Polly is now 93, a resident of the Kendal community in Lexington. She is my godmother, we are much alike in our tastes and dispositions, and she is one of my favorite people. We have lunch together every couple of weeks, and share a passion for gin martinis and a love for my mother, who was her only sister.

Another lifelong friend with whom I shared childhood, special-education teacher and writer Patty Pullen, has what she calls "velvet dreams," which she says are significantly different from her usual dreams. In one she saw (but did not interact with) her grandmother —whom she'd known only as an old and irritable woman forced to lived with her daughter and her daughter's family almost as a servant—as a beautiful girl dressed in a white turn-of-the-century nightdress. Still, Patty immediately knew it was her grandmother.

Stories like this one convince me that there's a world of evidence that the dead still have interest in the living, and that at least part of what happens when people die is that they stay connected to living loved ones through some kind of mutual vibration, for which the only word I can think of is *love*.

Sandy Harralson, while running Oak Spring Farm, a bed-and-breakfast near Fairfield, Virginia, recalls a time that her teenaged daughter Amy was feeling adolescently sad one afternoon and went to take a nap. Later Amy emerged from her room to announce that she had been visited by an elderly man who had made her feel much better. Her mother found it interesting, but shrugged it off, thinking her daughter had fallen asleep and had a dream.

Several weeks later, when the family visited Sandy's aging mother in another state, Amy happened to be looking through an old box of photos. Suddenly she pulled one out and exclaimed, "This is the man who was in my room!"

It was Amy's grandfather, Sandy's father, dead since before Amy was born. The house, incidentally, is the same one in which the Weilbachers experienced their Indian chief.

Sally Mann, the world-famous photographer, lives in Lexington. Before her father Bob Munger, a local doctor, died, he chose to be cremated. According to Sally, Dr. Munger had often joked that he would reincarnate as a crow. At the interment of his ashes at a private ceremony on his beautiful estate, Sally decided to photograph the family with the urn of ashes. She wanted to be in the picture herself, so she had an assistant slide one loaded plate into the camera, snap the first photograph, then slide in the second plate, and snap the second photograph.

When the pictures were developed, one was perfect. But the other had a shape of light above the funeral urn that looks for all the world like an ethereal crow, wings spread, rising out of the urn. Sally, a disbeliever, thinks there must have been some tear in the photographic plate that let in light. She subsequently discarded both plates. But some of her friends who remember Dr. Bob Munger's threat to return as a crow disagree with her conclusion.

At the house in Rockbridge Baths which my son Cochran lived in for several years, Raleigh, a friend of his, camps out for awhile from time to time. Raleigh tells me that three times his guitar, propped by his bed, has played itself in the night. At first he woke up to the sound of strings being plucked, thinking it might be the house rabbit that roams at night, or even the blacksnake that inhabits the attic, and sometimes comes downstairs. But when he turned on the light, there was nothing, just random strings having been plucked, notes still vibrating in the air.

The second night, he was awakened again, and turned on the light to see the strings moving, but no agent. For a few minutes he listened to notes that, he says, were almost a tune.

The third night it happened, he sat and watched the guitar play itself, a coherent but evanescent tune. He isn't a believer in ghosts; in fact, he totally rejects that explanation.

But here's what's interesting: when we bought the house, the previous owner told us that the family always thought that one room in the house was haunted—and it's the room where Raleigh sleeps.

Last time my friend Tenney Mudge, inventor of the Keepsafe Break-Away collar for dogs, and I were having lunch, she asked me what I was writing, and when I told her about this book, said matter-of-factly that she had an "apparent" ghost story. Picture her house at the top of a hill which goes down sharply in back to a creek. Across the creek on the ascending hill is a small, old cemetery near her barn, which stands more or less opposite her house. One afternoon when she crossed the creek to feed the horses, she noticed they were acting strange, on alert, facing the cemetery. Tenney turned, saw smoke hovering over the cemetery, assumed something was on fire, and went racing to the barn for two buckets. Calling across the creek for her then-husband Michael to come, she ran back down the hill to the creek for water, and began lugging the two sloshing buckets uphill. Meanwhile, Michael caught up with her, grabbing one of the heavy water buckets. He too saw the smoke over the cemetery.

However, when they got to the cemetery, Tenney says, there was no smoke, not even the smell of smoke. It hadn't drifted away; it was just gone. A survey of the cemetery proved that nothing was, or had been, on fire. There was no fog in the area. There's never been an explanation.

At a party, I see Elizabeth (Wassell) Sauder, a delightful artist, and someone I haven't seen in a long time. She asks what I'm writing, I tell her, and immediately she says, "I had a ghostly experience as a child, before I could read. I was about four. Everyone called me Buffy then. My family had moved into a dank old house I didn't like much. One night I woke up and there was a woman standing at the end of the bed who told me that she had the same name as me, *Elizabeth*, and told me her last name. She said she used to live in the house, and that it was a nice house, a happy house, and I shouldn't be afraid. I told my mother all this the next day.

"Some months later, while looking at an old scrapbook we'd found in the attic, I saw the woman's photograph and said to Mother, 'That's the lady who came into my room that night.' Under the woman's picture was the name I'd told my mother, which I still couldn't read."

Elizabeth's mother, Barbara Wassell Goldsten, confirmed her child's story from nearly half a century ago, adding that when Buffy told her about the visitor, she'd commented, "What a nice dream you had!"

She still remembered that Buffy had answered, "It wasn't a dream! She was right there at the end of my bed!"

Years ago at our house, we may have had a brief haunting by a cat we adored who got run over and killed during an ice storm. Thomas was still only a kitten, not yet a year old; he had one toy he especially liked, a small rag dog. I'd put some catnip into a slit in its tummy and sewn it up again, and Thomas loved to carry it around, hold it in his paws while he slept, and lick it.

For six mornings after his death, I found that toy lying in the dining room doorway just where I had to walk to get to the kitchen. Each morning I picked it up and tossed it back in the cat toy basket, assuming one of the other cats had dragged it out (still the most obvious explanation). About the third or fourth day it occurred to me that I'd never seen any of the other cats play with that toy, only Thomas. Yet I was finding it in the doorway each morning. For two more days it appeared there, and then not any more. Was Thomas letting me know he was still "somewhere" playing?

Ethan Bedell is a young Lexington friend in my aerobics class and dance company. One morning, he said he'd heard I was writing about psychic matters, and asked if he could tell me his story. So we met for lunch, and he did.

Ethan and his mother are intuitively close. Ethan also adored his maternal grandmother. While he was at Episcopal High School, his grandmother got sick and eventually died in a nursing home that happened to be near the school. On the night before she died, Ethan was able to tell her of his love and stroke her hand, though she was comatose by then.

The next morning when he learned of her death, he didn't know what else to do except go through the motions of his classes, sports, meals, the usual school day. He felt hugely sad. He turned down offers by his teachers to let him skip a class or take a test later. He felt that routine would keep him from flying apart.

Ethan is a cross-country runner; and so, late in the afternoon, he ran his usual course through the woods near Episcopal High. Suddenly, as he rounded a turn, thinking sadly of his grandmother, there in front of him right by the path were a patch of daffodils where there had been none the day before. Immediately he connected them with his grandmother, feeling that somehow they were "from her." He didn't know why, but he felt comforted.

That night, he told his mother, Meredith, on the phone about the daffodils. "That's odd," his mother said. "Remember how she used to quote the poem about daffodils?"

"No," said Ethan. He didn't remember at all.

"Yes," his mother insisted. "Your grandmother loved that Wordsworth poem: *I wandered lonely as a cloud/ That floats on high o'er vales and hills,/ When all at once I saw a crowd,/ A host, of golden daffodils...*"

The morning I mentioned writing this book to my friend of sixty-five years and frequent walking partner "Tut," she told me a story that happened soon after her father's death.

Colonel Tutwiler, a professor of English at VMI, died after a number of years of living in a local retirement community. The New Yorkers who bought his house when he could no longer stay alone in it are named McMillan, and Tut knew them only as the buyers of her family home.

A few months later, she ran into Mrs. McMillan at a church bazaar, and Mrs. McMillan said there was something she wanted to tell her, but in private.

At their meeting, Mrs. McMillan revealed that the McMillan's son and daughter-in-law had been staying at the house recently, when both of them woke up in the night hearing a man's voice calling out what they agreed sounded like, JoAnn? JoAnn? and "male" footsteps ascending the spiral stairs just inside the front door. Upon turning on lights, searching the premises, they found nothing.

"The funny thing was," Mrs. McMillan went on, "we heard from a friend the next day that your father had died the previous night. And what I wanted was to ask you is, was your mother's name by any chance JoAnn?"

Tut replied, "No, her name was Ann, same as mine." Then she thought about why "JoAnn" sounded so familiar to her also. "But Mother's sewing room was upstairs, and Father always came upstairs when he came home from VMI, looking for my mother, calling, *Oh, Ann! Oh, Ann?*"

Conde Glasgow Feddeman, widow of a Lexington physician Fred Feddeman, and a Lexington native, was in New York near the beginning of World War II, to be her best friend's maid-of-honor. The night before the wedding, she was rooming with her friend; and just after they had turned out the lights, Conde could see a young woman standing by the bride's bed, with long, black, wavy hair and a white gown with wide, lacy sleeves, her back to Conde. Conde rose onto her elbow and called out her friend's name. At that, the woman walked towards the door and disappeared into the darkness.

It struck her as so normal that Conde just turned over and went back to sleep, and never thought to even mention it to her friend the next day. The wedding went off as planned, her friend left on her honeymoon, and Conde went home.

Twenty-five years passed. At some point, when she and her friend met for a visit, her friend having divorced and remarried, it occurred to Conde that she'd never told her friend what she'd seen the night before her first wedding.

So she began the story, and her friend interrupted to say, "Oh, did she have those lacy, big sleeves on her dress?"

"Yes," Conde said. "So you saw her too!"

"Not then," her friend said. "But I did later."

Conde's friend went on to say she'd seen the apparition twice, once about a year after she was married. She woke one night in their Washington, D.C., apartment, to find the woman standing by her bed. She woke her husband to share this unexpected curious visit. His reaction was abject terror and physical nausea, which she found odd, because she felt only curious about it.

About a year after that event, when they were living on the west coast, it happened again, and again her husband woke up and was absolutely terrified. Conde's friend found the figure comforting, and could not understand her husband's uncontrollable fear.

Then she said to Conde, "Funny, after I divorced Charles, I never saw the ghost again. Hadn't thought of it til now."

The ghost had been no one she recognized. Conde told me that she wondered aloud if the ghost had been a protector, perhaps come the night before her wedding hoping to somehow dissuade her from her decision to marry a man who turned out to be the wrong partner—and periodically thereafter until her decision to divorce him. That might explain the husband's extreme reaction both times. It is notable that the vision appeared in three different localities, so it seems to have been attached to Conde's friend instead of the more usual attachment to place that ghosts seem to favor.

Shortly after her mother's death, Naomi Chadwick was in a nearly empty parking lot late one night, getting into a car with a man. She heard her dead mother's voice clearly, yelling, "Naomi!"

She looked around, truly expecting to see her mother, then blew it off as a figment of her imagination as she clicked back to the reality of her mother's death. A little later, the car wrecked, and in retrospect, she thinks her mother had been trying to warn her.

Naomi's sister Natalie Chadwick moved here with her family from Pennsylvania, and I met her by asking her about her license plate one day at the Post Office, which read UFOTRKER. (I'll save her UFO stories for another book.)

She hadn't lived here long, in a cabin she found west of Lexington, when she met her present husband Don Montgomery. She'd felt a male presence behind her house since moving in with her children and her Dad, but it was neutral and not bothersome.

Then she met Don. The first night he visited her, he asked her, "Who's the guy standing in the backyard in old-timey clothes?" When she explained, Don decided the thing to do was invite the presence in to the house. Practical jokes began; Natalie's daughter would say, "I feel people in here." While in the shower, Natalie would often feel a "pressing sensation" against the shower curtain, though she could see nothing. Once in the hallway outside the bathroom, something pinched her on the bottom, but no one was there. She had a feeling that he, the presence, was "ornery."

Things escalated when Don was home: soda caps flew around the room, there would be loud knocks at the door, and no one there when the door was opened.

Once when Natalie was home sick with flu, something grabbed her arm and shook it, waking her up. That time, the invisible presence felt helpful to her. But in general he came to feel to Natalie "possessive," and every time a male came to the house the force seemed to get stronger.

So Don eventually went around the house and dis-invited the presence, and it went away. Reasonable ghost!

My paternal grandfather, Greenlee D. Letcher, an attorney and the most genial and open-minded man who ever lived, was *willing* to believe in ghosts. He had graduated from VMI in 1886, kept up a lifetime friendship with the institution, and lived three houses from it on Letcher Avenue in Lexington. He told me he didn't think he'd ever seen a ghost, but then he hesitated, recalled that he'd seen a fire ball roll across the VMI parade ground once around sunset while he was taking his constitutional, and reckoned that it *might* have been his brother Hootie who'd recently died. Hootie was a New Market cadet who survived that slaughter at the age of fifteen, and lived to become a judge. The fireball would not allow my grandfather to get near it, he said.

It is strange to have learned from my Aunt Polly Curry, after my mother's death, that both my parents' families had experienced occurrences of a paranormal nature. These days Aunt Polly and I meet often for lunch. Polly easily accepts the paranormal, for she has experienced many unexplainable things in her life. For instance, in California during World War II when her husband was overseas, she found it hard to find any place to live on the west coast. Thus, she felt lucky to find a furnished apartment that had been owned by a woman who had just died. Polly moved right in to wait for her husband Lamar's return from the Pacific. She says she never felt welcome there, felt "disapproval" of her using the dead woman's toaster or bath mats or bed linens. Feeling lucky to have found any place to live, Polly ignored her feelings.

There was an ugly wall hanging in the living room that Polly hated. But she couldn't bring herself to take it down. One day her cousin Tootie visited her, and before she'd been in the apartment ten minutes, Tootie said anxiously, "Polly, what's behind the wall hanging?"

"Oh, nothing!" said Polly, thinking it an odd question. They lifted it and looked, and sure enough, nothing. But then Tootie wanted to leave the room, saying she felt uncomfortable there—she felt *someone was watching her* from behind the wall hanging. That Tootie felt as uncomfortable as she did confirmed Polly's uneasiness about the apartment. As soon as she could, she found somewhere else to live.

Looking back with a more open mind, I recall how, at nineteen, I may have experienced a ghost—though if I'd known it for a ghost, I'd have been terrified. And I was half-asleep, and unable to prove that what I experienced ever happened.

2

The Ghost of Anna Marie

It was early June of 1957, that lazy gap between end-of-classes at Hollins College and exams, when I was supposed to be studying, but instead I borrowed a car and with my friend Jane drove to Virginia Beach. On the way, we visited a classmate's house in Suffolk, Virginia. Ann Rollings lived in the old house with her younger sister and her parents. Jane stayed in Ann's room with her, while I drew the guest room.

In the night I awoke to find a thunderstorm going on, and a woman putting my windows down. I went immediately and gratefully back to sleep. In the morning, the windows were again open.

At breakfast, I thanked my hostess' mother for so kindly closing and re-opening my window. She said she hadn't been in my room. Nor, it turned out, had any other female in the house. What did the woman look like? they asked. I admitted that I couldn't say, that I hadn't exactly *seen* her.

Then maybe it was Dudley, they said. That was Ann's father.

But no, I was positive it had been a woman, though I could not say why. And that was when they said, *Maybe it was our ghost.* My hostess and her mother stared at each other as the hair on the back of my neck rose.

Here is their story: Ann's younger sister Rusty had beautiful red curly hair. One day when she was four, and eating breakfast, she announced to her mother that she had a different name. The lady in the picture over the mantel had talked to her. "She said *my* name's Anna Marie, and I was named for her."

The portrait was of the great-aunt for whom the child had indeed been named. Still, her mother thought, any number of people could have told the child that. Virginians have been known to talk about their ancestors.

Rusty's mother, father, and big sister were all pretty sure they'd never told little Rusty about the lady in the portrait and her connection. The child was quite steadfast: she insisted that the lady in the picture was the one who told her!

On a day sometime later, a new housekeeper told Mrs. Rollings that a woman was waiting to see her in the living room. Since the maid was rather new, Ann's mother didn't question her about who it was, and went to the living room. Empty.

Puzzled, she called in the maid, who was as baffled as Mrs. Rollings. "She was sitting right there when I came in," the maid insisted. "I didn't let her in. She was sitting right on the sofa and asked to see you."

"What did she look like?" came the inevitable question. The housekeeper allowed that she was sort of funny-looking, come to think of it: old-fashioned dress, all the way down to the floor; a big hat with a veil over the face; oh -- and long red hair, she added. "Matter of fact," she said, "she looked right much like that lady in the portrait over the mantel."

Guests also occasionally apparently encountered her: "Who was the lady in the long dress I just passed on the stairs?" one asked. "I just saw a woman looking out of the window on the landing while I was coming up the walk," another said. The lady was always red-haired, young, and dressed in long black clothes. No one ever seemed to think they had seen a ghost.

The house had been passed down on Ann's mother's side, and Anna Marie had been engaged to a man who went off to fight in the War Between the States. He, like so many others, never returned.

Eventually Anna Marie contracted consumption and died, still a spinster.

The house continued in the family, the people living in it aware of its history. But eighty years or more passed before the red-headed lady spoke to Rusty from the portrait and then appeared on subsequent occasions.

I was never able to recall any prior discussion about the supernatural with Ann. But in the two years I'd known her I could have heard her say she lived in a house with a ghost, then shelved the information in the back of my brain—until my visit triggered a memory I didn't know I had. Of course, I never did believe I'd encountered a ghost—just a thoughtful lady closing the windows for an overnight guest.

The grownups in that house took it seriously. They believed in their ghost. As I was then, I "decided" that it was just my imagination.

3

The Greenbrier Ghost (1985)

I never lost my fascination for ghost stories. In 1983 my dear friend Paul Shue, who had helped me write a book about train wreck songs, happened to mention that a relative of his had killed a girl, and that the girl's ghost had told on him, revealed him as the murderer. The events happened in West Virginia at the end of the nineteenth century. Interesting enough to try to get a book out of it, I decided, and so I did the research, interviewed a great many people, and wrote *The Man Who Wanted Seven Wives*. I solved the mystery of the so-called ghost to my satisfaction. Today, I might reach a different conclusion than I did back then. Briefly, here is the story.

The state roadside marker commemorating the event a few miles west of Lewisburg, West Virginia, right where Interstate 64 crosses old Route 60, ends by declaring that it's the "only known case in which (the) testimony from (a) ghost helped convict a murderer."

The briefest form of the story is that told by the road marker: "Interred in nearby cemetery is Zona Heaster Shue. Her death in 1897 was presumed natural until her spirit appeared to her mother to describe how she was killed by her husband Edward. Autopsy on the exhumed body verified the apparition's account. Edward, found guilty of murder, was sentenced to state prison."

Near the end of January 1897, Zona Heaster Shue, who had been a popular young girl in Greenbrier County, and was now a bride of three months, was found dead at the bottom of the stairs leading to the second floor of the log house where she lived with her new husband. Mrs. Shue's body was discovered by a neighbor, a black child of eleven who did chores for her, who ran to find a doctor.

Her body was taken the fourteen miles across the valley to her childhood home on Little Sewell Mountain, and buried three days later. At the time, there was no intimation in the local newspaper, *The Greenbrier Independent*, of anything unusual about the young woman's death. The physician who examined the body, Dr. George W. Knapp, announced that she "died of an everlasting faint." On January 30, however, he wrote in the death record book in nearby Lewisburg that she died of childbirth.

The Richlands section of Greenbrier County, just west of Lewisburg, West Virginia, is aptly named, being an area of fertile fields, rolling hills, cattle farms. Then, it was a remote area, and the people were clannish. The Shue woman's husband was not one of them, but a blacksmith from Pocahontas, the next county to the north. Edward "Trout" Shue had moved to Greenbrier recently, and from the beginning cut a wide swath, as he was from all reports good-looking and powerful, charismatic and braggity, and he attracted even more notice than most strangers. Furthermore, he had swept off her feet one of their own, and married her faster than anyone could say Jack Robinson.

Within a month of her untimely death, the dead girl's mother was telling people in the neighborhood that Zona's spirit had appeared to her four nights in a row to accuse the blacksmith of her violent death, and to instruct her mother to "Tell on him!" to set the record straight about her dying. Word spread quickly that Mary Jane Heaster was convinced by these visions that the husband, who called himself Edward, but was really named Erasmus Stribbling Trout Shue, called Trout, had killed her daughter, whom Mrs. Heaster had not seen since their wedding on October 20.

In the weeks that followed Mrs. Shue's death, there was a great deal of local gossip about the glamorous blacksmith, and some details of his past that he had neglected to share with his new neighbors came to light. Not only had he changed his name, he also failed to mention that Zona was not his first wife, nor even his second. Shue's first marriage, to Allie Estelline Cutlip, in 1885, had produced a child, Girta Lucretia, and ended in divorce four years later, while Shue was in the state penitentiary serving time for horse stealing.

A clergyman who had been sought out in the middle of the night to officiate at that wedding, a Methodist circuit rider named R.R. Little, stepped forward at the time of Zona Shue's death to relate a bizarre story of going to marry the young couple in 1885 at the groom's home, having been summoned there by Trout Shue himself. He reported the groom's arrival, not in early afternoon as planned, but at midnight, with a marriage license from the wrong county. The Reverend Little told how Trout himself insisted that they all march a mile to the county line and the couple be married there in the middle of the night. The Reverend Little refused firmly, and left. The young couple were married by another clergyman the next day in the county where the license had been issued.

Estie and Trout went to live with her parents. But Shue reportedly beat his wife so badly that a vigilante group of men in the neighborhood jerked him out of bed one winter night and threw him through the ice into a deep hole in the Greenbrier River near where he lived, as a warning. Estie took her husband's side, begging the neighbors to let him alone, even hitting at them with boards during this episode. The Shues became parents to a baby girl in February 1887, and it is not clear whether the mob appeared before or after her birth.

In December of 1888 *The Pocahontas Times* reported that Trout Shue was in jail, where he stayed until his conviction for horse stealing the following April. He served time in the state pen until December 20, 1890. A divorce decree, issued while he was in the state prison, states, "He without any cause abandoned and deserted me. He said he wanted me to leave him. I said to him that I was not going to do any such thing, and he took his property away and threw what I have out of the house..."

In June of 1894, Trout Shue was married again, this time to Lucy Ann Tritt, from nearby Alderson. They lived with his parents on Droop Mountain near Hillsboro, where Lucy died less than eight months later. *The Pocahontas Times* stated only that she died suddenly. There was no investigation. Four entirely different stories were told of her death, but not at the time—only later, when Shue was under suspicion of murdering Zona, his third wife. He had moved down to Greenbrier from Pocahontas in the autumn of 1896, and soon thereafter had married Zona Heaster.

Eventually his mother-in-law, by all accounts an extremely devout woman, visited The Honorable John Alfred Preston, the prosecuting attorney of the county. Though there remains no record of that visit, Mrs. Heaster must have presented enough troubling information that the result was a court order for the exhumation of Zona's corpse and an autopsy upon the body of Zona, her only daughter among eight children.

When a healthy young woman died in those days, childbirth was usually the presumed cause. People coming to view the corpse had found it odd that Zona Shue's head was so loose that stuffing, specifically a pillow and a folded sheet, had been placed in the coffin to keep the head upright. Some folks noticed some discoloration on the right cheek. All noticed that Shue himself kept jealous watch over the body, and would let no one near. Dr. Knapp had been treating Zona for some time prior to her death, and his listing of "childbirth" as the cause of death would certainly point to the probability that Zona was pregnant when she died.

Newspaper accounts say it was "certain citizens" who grew suspicious, which does not preclude Mrs. Heaster, but includes others as well. Prosecuting attorney Preston went himself out to the Richlands section to see Dr. Knapp, who had examined the corpse. Knapp admitted that because the husband had exhibited such distress over anyone's touching her, his examination on the day her body was found had been sketchy. Furthermore, Trout Shue had already dressed his wife himself, before Knapp got there, in a high-necked gown, with a big scarf around the neck.

The prosecuting attorney must also have talked with other people in the area. Preston and Knapp together agreed that an autopsy would clear things up, confirming or refuting the suspicions Mrs. Heaster—and by then others—had voiced, and allow Knapp to know better how Zona had died. Of equal importance, an autopsy would lift suspicion from the blacksmith if indeed he were innocent.

Obviously, haste was necessary. An exhumation was ordered, an inquest jury assembled, and the day appointed. They chose Nickell School House for convenience, as it was close by Soule Methodist Church, in the yard of which Zona had been buried. The school children were told not to come to school for the day. Three physicians would participate in the posthumous examination.

Thirty-one days after it had been buried, the body of Zona Shue was again brought to light, because "rumors in the community" had caused the local authorities "to suspect that she may not have died from natural causes." *The Greenbrier Independent* went on to editorialize: "…her husband, E.S., commonly known as Trout Shue, was suspected of having brought about her death by violence or in some way unknown to her friends." It reported that "Shue vigorously complained, but it was made clear to him that he would be forced to go to the inquest if he did not go agreeably. He said on the way that he knew he would come back under arrest. Then he added, "But they will not be able to prove I did it."

Shue reportedly sat in the corner of the schoolhouse on a bale of hay during the three hours that the autopsy took. Because they did not know what they were looking for, they first examined the corpse's stomach for poison.

If it seems odd that the broken neck of the corpse was not detected immediately, modern physicians assert that all corpses have floppy heads, as all the muscles are relaxed and the head is extremely heavy in relation to the rest of the body. In fact, it is not uncommon for a corpse's neck to be broken merely by moving it without supporting the head, according to pathologists.

Newspapers reported that at the end, the doctors, working around Zona's head and neck, suddenly began to whisper together. Then one of them turned to the man on the bale of hay and said, "Well, Shue, we have found your wife's neck to have been broken." *The Pocahontas Times* of March 9 was specific: "On the throat were the marks of fingers indicating that she had been choken." The examination disclosed "that the neck was dislocated between the first and second vertebrae. The ligaments were torn and ruptured. The windpipe had been crushed at a point in front of the neck."

The autopsy report, published in the paper, ends with a statement that would seem to contradict the popular rumor of Zona's having been pregnant at the time of her death, "All other portions and organs of the body [with the exception of the neck] were apparently in a perfectly healthy state." The results were made public at once. Shue was charged with murder and jailed in Lewisburg to await trial.

John Alfred Preston and his assistant prosecutor, Henry Gilmer, now had to build a case against Shue as the murderer of his wife. Shue for his part continued to say from jail, "They will not be able to prove I did it." He was defended by William Parkes Rucker and James P.D. Gardner, court-appointed attorneys. Their efforts to gather witnesses, alibis, or other testimonials to his innocence, must have been discouraging, for on May 20, 1897, *The Greenbrier Independent* reported that "Trout Shue …now in jail awaiting trial for the murder of his wife, has threatened to kill himself."

On June 17, the same paper reported that Shue had had 120 witnesses summoned, though a law order exists for the summoning of one only, one of his brothers, J.P. Shue. On June 25, 1897, *The Pocahontas Times* reported, "On the issue of this trial depends the question of whether Shue, who is a Droop citizen, will reach his seventh wife, as he has boasted he would have seven. The passing of the third endangers his neck or is liable to send him to the penitentiary where there is no marrying or giving in marriage."

The trial began on Wednesday, June 23, 1897. The county law orders are maddeningly vague, saying for each day of the trial only that E.S. Shue was that day led to the bar in custody of the jailer, and that the jury "having heard the evidence in part" were at the end of the day "once more committed to the care and custody of the sheriff of this county and his deputies…"

The trial began with the prosecuting attorney making an opening statement. Preston explained to the jury that the case against Shue was entirely circumstantial, but that the evidence was "such as had never been presented in any court before." It has since been assumed, in the absence of the transcript, which disappeared from the courthouse in the early nineteen-thirties, that Preston referred to the ghost story.

But in fact, the ghost story was not referred to in any of the summings-up at all. Quite likely, all Preston meant was that he had so great a wealth of circumstantial evidence that the blacksmith would be convicted on the basis of that evidence, lacking direct proof that he had murdered his wife. Although a murder conviction based on circumstantial evidence was not unheard of, it was extremely rare.

Dr. George Knapp, the first witness for the state, revised both his early conclusions. "An everlasting faint" tells us only that he had no idea what killed her. His second conclusion, the one in the Greenbrier death record — death by childbirth — points to a wrong but logical assumption based on what had ailed Zona the last month of her life.

"The evidence… makes it quite clear that Mrs. Shue did not commit suicide," the *Independent* stated.

"The postmortem made it clear that her neck had been dislocated but there was no mark upon her person to suggest or other evidence to show that she had subjected herself to any sort of violence." Thus *The Greenbrier Independent* neatly and delicately addresses the issue of pregnancy or attempted abortion. "Others testified that Shue was the only person seen or known to have been on (his) premises prior to finding Mrs. Shue dead."

The question that is central to the story of the Greenbrier Ghost is whether it was in fact the ghost story that led to the jury's decision to find Shue guilty of murder. All present had heard that a ghost was involved in this trial, and they assumed that Mrs. Heaster would tell about it. Thus when she was called to the stand, there was undoubtedly renewed excitement among the observers as well as the jury. Mrs. Heaster was a leading state witness; her suspicions were the seed that had grown into the murder trial of her son-in-law. And Thomas Dennis, editor of *The Greenbrier Independent*, knew it would make sensational copy.

The ghost testimony is the only part of the trial transcript we have today, as it was printed in *The Greenbrier Independent*. Mrs. Heaster told an impassioned story about speaking four nights in a row with her dead daughter, of Zona's telling her of a fight preceding the murder because "she had fixed no meat for supper," of Shue's wringing her neck and throwing her downstairs.

The "ghost testimony" was brought out by the defense. Surely it would seem strange for the defense to have voluntarily called up a hostile witness, the mother of the dead girl, who had the most compelling reasons of anyone for hating their client!

What we can assume is that Prosecutor Preston, not the defense, first called Mrs. Heaster to the stand, only as the mother of the dead girl and the first person to call his attention to the fact that there were reasons to believe that Zona's death had not been natural. But all Preston would have questioned her about was what she'd taken to him—suspicion. We may fairly assume that it was her and others' suspicions, and not the tale of the spectral appearance of the dead girl, that had led to the autopsy.

Preston wanted to demonstrate to the jury that Mrs. Heaster was sane and reliable, and had not set a trap for her son-in-law. He skirted the ghost story because it would have made his witness seem unreliable, and also because it was basically inadmissible evidence, being hearsay, or secondhand.

The defense also knew the ghost story was inadmissible; it seems obvious that Rucker in bringing up the ghost was trying to discredit what Preston had been trying to establish: Mary Jane Heaster's sound and sane character. The newspaper printed her ghost testimony, which by then included some information that seemingly came from the autopsy. The testimony, though devoutly made and sworn to be the truth, shows pre-judgment on Mrs. Heaster's part against Shue, and includes details not known until the published autopsy results, such as the fact that there was no meat in Zona's stomach at the time of death.

Shue, a clever fellow described repeatedly as a braggart, had spent some time in prison earlier in his life, and may have studied the law with other inmates who were trying to win appeals and new trials. He reportedly seemed confident throughout the trial that they "will not be able to prove I did the killing." Rucker and Gardner may have assured Shue there could be no conviction. For at the end, Shue himself took the stand, rambled on for an entire afternoon, and "appealed to the jury to look into his face and then say if he was guilty." This made, according to the *Independent* account, an "unfavorable impression."

In concluding its report of the trial, the *Independent* carefully repeats, "So the connection of the accused with the crime depends entirely upon the strength of the circumstantial evidence introduced by the state." The state did not introduce the ghost story. A nearby paper, *The Monroe Watchman*, reported that "Shue was all the time laboring under the impression that he could not be convicted on circumstantial evidence, and felt secure in knowing there was no witness but himself to the crime."

The jury returned a verdict of guilty after only one hour and ten minutes of deliberation. The accounts in *The Greenbrier Independent* make clear that Shue was convicted of the murder of his third wife on circumstantial evidence, and not because of a "ghost's testimony." He was sentenced to life in the state prison. Following a foiled lynching attempt a few days later, Shue was taken by train to the state prison in Moundsville, where he died on the first of March, 1900. While in prison, he executed a strange haunting drawing, which the present owner, a woman in her late eighties, says was sent to her father who owned the smith shop where Shue was employed while in Greenbrier. She says it accompanied a letter in which Shue identified the subjects as himself and Zona. In the drawing are two people and two coffins floating above their heads. The smaller coffin, hers—perhaps "her case"—is drawn closed; but his "case" is still open.

Believing back in 1985 in a rational world where the dead stay dead, I wondered where Mrs. Heaster got the ghost story, and why she invented or dreamed up such a thing. Why wasn't the suspicion of the neighbors combined with her own misgivings enough to take to the prosecuting attorney? Why did she need the drama of a ghost? In fact, Mrs. Heaster lived until 1916 and never recanted her story. As far as I could learn, her husband remained silent on the matter until his death in 1917.

My assumption finally was that Mrs. Heaster, Zona's mother, knew the blacksmith was clever, unprincipled, and persuasive. If he'd murdered once, he might murder again. So to accuse him directly would have been rash. If the law took no notice of her accusations, he might prove to be extremely dangerous to her in the future.

So pretending to receive the news directly from Zona, Mrs. Heaster thought to appeal to the superstitions of her mountaineer neighbors and get a lot of public attention. A ghost story was more arresting than mere suspicion. As it turned out, she didn't need the ghost story, for Shue was convicted, according to every account, strictly on earthly, not unearthly, considerations.

My research was more or less complete. I was satisfied that the ghost story was merely an ingenious method by which a canny country woman contrived to get the attention she felt was merited. I felt too that the Greenbrier populace turned out to be more sophisticated, less gullible, than she had given them credit for. Then came, belatedly, a call from Fred Long, the editor of *The Hinton News-Leader*, whom I'd visited with early in my search for information. It was fairly late at night; he called to see how my book was progressing. As I talked with him, he made some reference I didn't understand, to "the other ghost story." Puzzled, I asked him to explain.

"I mean the one in the paper on the day she was buried," Fred said. "Surely you've seen that."

I thought I had read every word of those old newspapers in the preceding two years. By then I knew what medicines people were taking, what houses and coffins and coffee cost. I had read the Gothic short stories that were common in the papers of the day; I had even thought *they* must have been instrumental in putting the idea of a ghostly appearance into Mrs. Heaster's head.

But the one story I'd missed appeared on January 28, 1897, in the same paper that on page three had reported Zona's death. On page one the following story appeared, thus solving to my satisfaction the origin of the story of the Greenbrier Ghost.

> A Ghost Story.—J. Henneker Heaton tells in the London Literary World an interesting sequel to the most famous Australian ghost story, which came to his knowledge as one of the proprietors of the leading New South Wales weekly, "The Town and Country Journal." One of the most famous murder cases in Australia was discovered by the ghost of the murdered man sitting on the rail of a dam (Australian for horse pond) into which his body had been thrown. Numberless people saw it, and the crime was duly brought home.
>
> Years after, a dying man making his confession said that he invented the ghost. He witnessed the crime, but was threatened with death if he divulged it as he wished to, and the only way he saw out of the impasse was to affect to see the ghost where the body would be found. As soon as he started the story, such is the power of nervousness that numerous other people began to see it, until its fame

reached such dimensions that a search was made and the body found, and the murderers brought to justice.

The juxtaposition of these two apparently unrelated news stories goes far beyond the likelihood of coincidence. Mary Jane Heaster *obviously* saw this story and hoped that what happened in it would happen in Greenbrier to bolster her story, to keep Shue from seeing that it was she who accused him.

What I have wondered since being shown this story is why no one brought it up at the trial. For many others in the Greenbrier area must have read that story, too. But those Greenbrier folks were smart. They were not Appalachian rubes. Apparently they knew the circumstantial evidence against Shue was strong enough to convict him. Pointing out that Mary Jane Heaster was lying would only have muddied the waters. Surely the ends of justice have been served in stranger ways. But here, clearly, was the origin of the story of the ghostly visits of Zona Heaster Shue.

My research efforts resulted in *The Man Who Wanted Seven Wives*, Algonquian Books, 1986, reissued by Quarrier Books in 2000. I still think my explanation is probably the most likely one. But today, I would not be so adamant, for I now believe in ghosts, and I believe the living can communicate with the dead.

The world offers us a reason why rationalists can continue to ignore overwhelming evidence: for any ghost story, there can be at least one other possible explanation. But, for my money, not for all of them.

This story of the Greenbrier Ghost traveled as far as England. In 1897 the youngish Psychic Society of Great Britain (founded in 1882) sent two researchers all the way from London to West Virginia to take depositions from all who had been connected with the case. They concluded that the story of the Greenbrier Ghost remains one of the most impressive ghost stories in their files of nearly 150 years. I have seen the files in London. I now can believe, along with the trained British psychics, that Mrs. Shue may truly have received communication from her dead daughter.

4

Just Your Imagination?

When I complained once to a wise woman about thinking that visitations, abductions, dreams, seemed to me to be only products of the imagination, and that I was sure that my past-life regressions were *only my imagination*, she replied mildly, "Well, certainly. Who else's imagination would it be?" That answer to me was like a Zen koan, on the surface absurd. Yet Einstein wrote that imagination was more important than knowledge.

A nervous skinny kid, I was always asking when my parents were out of earshot, "Are there any ghosts in your house? You know any ghost stories?" I knew it embarrassed my parents—in the conservative, geocentric forties and fifties when I was growing up. I got the impression that maybe ignorant people believed such things, but we didn't. My grandfather, whom I called "Andaddy," was the only one even open to the possibility of anything beyond this life except Episcopal Heaven. He was a wide-open person generally.

By five, I already knew the truth about Santa. To my shame, I delighted in "educating" all the other kids I could. This did not prove conducive to my believing in out-of-the-ordinary experiences. I assumed from that time on that all unexplainable stories, like those about Santa, could be explained away. That became my framework, my "working hypothesis."

At ten, I joined the Rosicrucians. It was 1948, I was reading "Tales from the Crypt" and listening to hillbilly music, singing on a local radio station, listening to ghost stories at Girl Scout camp, and from the black folks that cooked in all my friends' kitchens. My mother didn't know what to do about me. The Rosicrucian promise was to connect their members with past lost wisdom, which I wanted so bad I could taste it—and it cost five dollars—five weeks' allowance for me. I made the sacrifice, read the material when it came, but as it had been made clear to me by the highest authorities, my parents, that all that stuff was nonsense, I slid away, easily convincing myself that I didn't believe any of it. I let my membership slide. Unfortunately, I can no longer remember all the ancient wisdom I tucked in back then.

In 1955, when we were allowed as high school seniors to choose our own topics for senior theses, it came naturally to me to choose witchcraft, white and black. I read Montague Summers on witchcraft and demonology, William B. Seabrook on witchcraft, werewolves, and vampires, C.G. Loomis on white magic, Newbell Niles Puckett on folk beliefs of southern Negroes, George Lyman Kittredge on New England witchcraft, Ralph Major on the healing power of faith, John Donne's *An Experiment in Time*, and Arthur Conan Doyle's *The Edge of the Unknown*. In that book, first published in 1930, there is an ironic sentence that begins, "In these days when the facts of psychic phenomena are familiar to all save those who are willfully ignorant …" I think we are not much farther along that path today than we were 75 years ago!

By the end of the year-long project culminating in my high school senior thesis of about 16 typed pages, I had concluded that the mind of the believer makes phenomena happen, good or evil; that black and white witchcraft were two faces of the power of suggestion. Black magic was destructive psychology, and white magic was benevolent, positive, helpful psychology. I got an A, and I thought I understood what "it" was all about. That information must be deeply internalized, for I know to this day that I do create my own reality by choosing how to react to whatever happens to me. No one can take away my choice of how to react.

In high school, we experimented with hypnotism. Some people were so easy to hypnotize it was ridiculous. My cousin Seymour Paul, who was about my age, was hypnotized one time at the school he attended, and told that every time he heard the word "school," he would squat down, cluck and squawk like a chicken. He was not properly brought back to normal-level consciousness, and he told me only recently (he's now over seventy) that for *years* afterwards, every time he heard the word "school," he had to fight the desire to squat down and make chicken-like noises.

I watched a blister rise on the finger of a boyfriend of mine named Mike Junkin under hypnosis who was told he'd burnt it on a cigarette.

I (and several other girls) were the objects of an experiment in a psychology class at Hollins College one day while I was a student there. In retrospect, I don't remember feeling bad at all until several people said to me throughout one day words to the effect that I looked sick. "Gee, are you feeling okay?" "You don't look so hot," another said. By day's end, I had checked into the infirmary with a fever. I was furious (and got well instantly) when I was told after supper that I'd been the subject of a suggestive experiment.

Those things all confirmed my theory of mind over matter—I saw that I and other people could be "fooled" by what we decided to believe, and believed that I could govern my own feelings by "deciding" to be, say, cheerful as opposed to sad or grumpy.

I tried the Catholics (well, if I was going to be a Christian, I'd go back to the *real* version of Christianity) my freshman year in college, but was politely dis-invited because I questioned too much, and argued endlessly. We never were a fit, Catholicism and I.

I investigated Judaism while dating a Jewish man, but my relationship with his faith ended when my relationship with him ended, though the Judaic faith made a lot more sense to me than Christianity. Virgin conception was pretty much what some of my pregnant classmates were claiming; and as to rising from the dead—well, clearly they just *thought* Jesus was dead. Obviously, he'd been in some kind of coma. (There's *always* another explanation, right?)

But more important, I couldn't square Christ's religion of love with things like the Crusades, the Spanish Inquisition, the conquest and methodical destruction of native Americans by Europeans, all in the name of Christianity—and the persistent prevalent treatment of minorities who, I thought, were as much God's children as I was. I left my own Episcopal church—rashly—one day after a member remarked to me following the service, "My, you cert'n'ly did look *white* sitting in the choir next to that *Nigger.*" The woman she so designated was, in fact, an opera singer from New York, and about a million times better than any of the rest of our voices in the choir.

For several decades I described myself as an existentialist and an agnostic (in part to prove what an intellectual I was, naturally). Then reason taught me that the world was too organized (I was learning plant taxonomy at the time) to be without a theological cause. So I became a *deist*, though without any conviction that the deity had any personal interest in me, or in any of us.

I had plenty of proof of Deity's non-involvement: certainly justice is meted out unfairly on every hand; I read the papers. A high school hoodlum, high on acid, totals his car and escapes without a scratch, while in another accident a drunk kills a young man on the verge of a brilliant adulthood, or three elderly women driving to church. Cancer is doled out randomly, to the good and the evil alike. Whatever final cause there is surely wasn't noticing the grieving children when a 37-year old friend of mine died of brain cancer.

In the world of Islam versus Christianity as I write this there appears, tragically, to be no stepping back from escalating conflict. So where is Deity in this? Absent? Bored? Malevolent? Dispassionate? Yet there must have been some intellectual genius that started everything in this complicated universe. How could anyone with even a smidgen of knowledge about science not believe in at least an Intelligence behind things?

There was always a lot to fuel my *disbelief* in things unseen. For instance, in the early summer of 1967, I read of a "glowing grave" in a cemetery in Crimora, Virginia, about fifty miles from Lexington. Hundreds of visitors to the Mt. Bethel EUB Church had seen it, and I wanted to. I gathered up some friends, and we made the trip one night. The glow was supposed to be the size of a basketball, brightest between ten and midnight, and speculation about what it might be ranged from a UFO to reflections of headlights. One newspaper account speculated that as the man in the grave had died of cancer, perhaps radiation from the body was seeping out and somehow causing the light.

With great difficulty, wrong turns and backtracking along narrow dirt roads, we didn't get there until after midnight. The cemetery was locked and surrounded by a high link fence, and any cars that might have been there earlier were now gone. Comparing the newspaper account—which showed the grave with an arrow pointing at it—we finally located the spot. Eventually one of my friends pointed, saying he was sure he'd seen a glow—right *there*. We all crowded around, stood where he stood pointing, peered into the gloom, and finally another said, "Oh, yes! I see it!" After a time, each one of us detected the subtle glow (it looked like a greenish lighted basketball-sized mist to me). Satisfied and shivering, we went home, awed by the experience—only to learn, the next day, that we had been at the wrong cemetery, several miles from the one with the glow. A writer friend, Rick Hite, translating poems from Spanish, coined the useful word "disencounters," and it seems to be the right word for what we had that night at the wrong cemetery: a *disencounter*.

The lesson of that trip has stayed with me: how easily we human beings "conjure" up images, persuade ourselves of something we want to see. That was fuel for my unbelief—which, as a form of belief, of course structured and informed my subsequent experiences. Carl Sagan was probably not the first to write that a lot follows from whatever it is you believe.

Anxious always to know the *truth*, I saved up all the disencounters firmly—probably while ignoring the synchronicities that were occurring in my life—if only I had noticed.

In high school I had a boyfriend named Mike Junkin with whom I tried an experiment after both of us had read *Peter Ibbetson* by George duMaurier. We planned to meet in spirit or in dreams, as the characters in that book do, one night at eleven at the State Drugstore in Lexington, where my friends and I gathered after school to drink cherry cokes. It was a narrow store, shotgun-style, one aisle from front to back. I went to sleep that night and dreamed I was in a booth in the middle of the store, and that Mike came in the back door, walked past me, and out the front. I told him about it the next day. He replied, "In my dream, I went in the back door and looked for you but did not see you, so I walked on out the front way." Because we had not "met" as intended, I decided our experiment was all rubbish, as fictional as the duMaurier novel. Today I might be willing to see it differently.

I saw colors around people's heads when I was little, and can still remember (though I can't see them anymore) what colors were around people I knew well. I learned much later that what I was doing was probably *synesthesia*—a mixing of senses—so that I was associating colors with characteristics that I thought people possessed, and endowing them with those meaning-laden colors. But some people would say I was seeing auras.

I was fascinated by Tibet, and I thought at the time that it was because of Lowell Thomas's 1949 visit there, short-waved to us in Lexington, Virginia, every night at six-thirty. But why did so many other subjects escape my attention, and Tibet catch my attention so thoroughly that by the time I was thirteen I had read every book in English about Tibet in all three libraries in my town? Now I've accessed a past lifetime spent as a skinny, hungry, cold, monk in Tibet who died only days before I was born—quite nearby where I was born, actually, in Peking, China.

My favorite poem when I was about ten—which I memorized—was called "Evolution" by Langston Smith. It balled up evolution with reincarnation. It made sense to me, so I believed it. In the poem a male and a female start out together as a tadpole and a fish in primordial slime, and then embark on a long journey as soul-mates for eternity, coming back slightly more evolved every go-round. In the end, they sit at Delmonico's sipping wine and wondering what their next step in reincarnation together will be.

The high school science I took dealt only with the reality of what we experience sensually—can see, measure, weigh, and replicate. I knew some things were so small they only appeared when we peered through the brass microscopes in the lab that always smelled of iodine. A world religion course taught me that Buddhists believe the exact opposite: that there is no objective reality at all. With a rationalist background, though, that was impossible to absorb. Was a thing true, or wasn't it? It had to be real or not, one way or the other. Period. The End. Didn't it?

Then, one day in May of 1996, I was able to collect three girlfriends from high school days to come to lunch at my house. My doing so was prompted by one Betty Agnor Bourne recognizing me in the grocery store those forty-plus years later, and our subsequent chat. I asked her to lunch, then found that two other friends from the old days, Patty Pullen and Lois Meade Burwell Hamric, were also free. We, of course, spent most of the time gabbing about high school days, beaus, and anecdotes. I was having a great time recalling my first love, the divine football hero and Student Government President Harry Bowes, who would, at 29, become the youngest college president in the United States.

Literally, as I was walking the last of them out to the sidewalk, behind me in the house the phone rang. It was none other than Harry Bowes, now a lobbyist living in Colorado. He said he'd just been *thinking about me*, and decided to call. I was clear-headed enough to think about confirmation, call out to Patty, who came back in and chatted briefly with Harry. I'd seen Harry twice since high school, when he came back to Lexington for short visits. But he'd never called me—in forty-one years! If it wasn't thoughts travelling, what else could it have been? Mere coincidence seems far too cavalier an explanation. That was not "just my imagination." I cherish *knowing* that some part of our minds can travel over long distances in no time at all.

5

Dreams

Sometimes humans are able to briefly pull aside whatever veil separates this level of existence from other realities. Some of the agents leading to these altered states are drugs, alcohol, self-inflicted pain, sensory isolation, starvation, listening to certain sounds such as drumming or meditating. But perhaps the commonest form of contact with other realities beyond space and time occurs in dreams.

Patty Scala, whom I met while she was tiling my bathroom, told me that in the early nineties she had a single, unsettling, extremely vivid dream. She and her husband were honeymooning in an inn called the Isaak Walton, possibly in Montana (she isn't sure what state they were in). In the dream she *was* an older woman in the company of a younger one, and the two women were with great satisfaction killing an older man and a young man, their plan being to drag them out to the nearby railroad track and make it appear that a train had run over them. She remembers the hot blood and brain matter splattering her face and arms, recalls the dress she wore, felt her shoes were too small and hurt her feet. She recalls the absolute *delight* in the killing, the getting even—and the sense that the younger woman was her daughter or daughter-in-law. Together they were wreaking vengeance for some dreadful wrong.

Next morning Patty told her husband she wanted to leave, telling him about the disturbing dream. The owner inquired if something was wrong, as they'd registered to stay two nights. She asked the owner if there was a history of a murder there.

"Nobody's been murdered," he said. "But there were two guys killed out there when the train ran over them, back in the twenties." Patty claims she has never had another psychic experience of any kind in her life.

Adeline Suthers of Buena Vista, Virginia, lost her husband in October of 1997. Since then she has been visited often in dreams by a man she describes as younger, taller, and much handsomer than her husband was, and yet she *knows absolutely that it is he*.

Barbara Wassell Goldsten was nursing her baby one night in her house on Brigantine Island, near Atlantic City, New Jersey, when it began to snow outside, and she fell into a sort of reverie, half-awake and half-dreaming. She had a most peculiar dream or vision: that the little grocery store where she traded was robbed by two men, and that they took cigarettes and money and then hid their booty in a washing machine. So odd was the dream that she told it to her husband at breakfast—who said, "Oh, what a crazy dream," and went off to work in the snow that had accumulated during the night.

Later in the morning she called the grocery store to ask them to deliver some things to her. The delivery boy arrived quite a bit later, with the apologetic remark, "Things have been crazy today. Someone robbed the store last night."

"What did they take?" she asked.

"Just cigarettes and money," the delivery boy replied. "The police have been there all day dusting for fingerprints, which has made us late with the deliveries."

"Do you have a washing machine in the store?" she asked.

"Why no, of course not."

"For what it's worth," she said, "the money and cigarettes are stowed inside a washing machine." She told the man about her dream, but he just shook his head doubtfully. As they discussed it, he remarked that the robbery had to have been before the snow, as there were no footprints.

Later when her husband came home, Barbara said, "Tell me what I told you I dreamed last night." He confirmed what she had told him, and she said, "It happened—and apparently I dreamed it as it happened. They stole exactly what I said." She says today that she thinks they never found the stolen goods, not in a washing machine, not anywhere else.

Her skeptical husband's response to this apparent clairvoyance was, "Pure coincidence!"

Burwell's new wife, Wafa Wingfield, who is Muslim, had a dream that left her terrified and hoping never to have another psychic experience.

Her father was suffering some kind of trouble, and she prayed to Allah for the trouble to be resolved. In the night, she was awakened by a hand on her shoulder shaking her roughly and a voice telling her to wake up. She recognized the voice as belonging to a janitor in the building where she worked, named David. He said, "What you asked, I will do in three days."

Wafa lay still, terrified, afraid to turn and look at this man she barely knew. Finally she went back to sleep.

Three days later, her father's trouble dissolved. Afterwards, she spoke to a Muslim priest, who told her that when the prophets answered prayers, they often came in the personas of persons bearing their names. So Wafa's prayer, she believes, was answered by the prophet David himself, who had to choose another David to manifest an earthly intervention. Nonetheless, Wafa found the experience very frightening.

I had an interesting dream just before my book about my grandparents' lives came out (*My Dearest Angel*, Ohio University Press, 2002). It was one morning about six. I had been a bit worried, now that the book was actually being published, about whether it was all right to publish my grandparents' private correspondence; this dream seemed to me to point to at least my grandfather's approval of my doing so. (I know my grandmother would *not* have been so willing.)

I dreamed that the time on my bedside clock was 1:06, when I went upstairs after lunch to the bedroom to look for something. There in the recliner by the bed sat my grandfather, his face plumper than I remembered, his hair still wispy and white, his face wreathed in pleasure. He looked sparkling and healthy. The recliner was on the opposite side of the bed than where it usually was.

In the dream I *knew* it was a dream, because Andaddy has been dead for nearly fifty years; but he looked so lifelike I asked him if I could hug him. He said yes, and I did, acutely aware of how narrow his shoulders were, and what a small man he was, and of his characteristic aura, musty with a touch of distant fried onion. That is how he always smelled to me.

He then said, using his old nickname for me, "Little Sweetheart, I brought you a present," and he reached into his coat (I could see he was wearing a vest), continuing, "It's some special wheat bread. It's right good."

I thought how like him to bring something plain but wholesome. As he reached into his coat and extracted a waxed-paper wrapped item, I awoke.

I puzzled about the symbolism of that whole wheat bread, tough and dense. I had been thinking of its plain-ness—and its superior nourishment—which could be said to be the gifts he in fact gave me.

The bread of life, a friend suggested. *Daily bread*, said another. At any rate, he was obviously pleased with me, which seemed to answer my concern about publishing the book.

I don't know if dreams represent real visits from people beyond death, but maybe that doesn't matter if it's as comforting to the dreamer as that dream was to me.

Another dream I had: my father, dead since 1994, was in his life a stock market wizard. In the summer of 2002, as the stock market fell farther each day, I asked him for advice one night as I went to sleep. It was a time when many investors were getting out of the market. That night, I had an odd dream: I was sitting on a forest path in autumn, with a fallen tree across my lap. I couldn't move. I wasn't hurt, and I wasn't afraid. From the side of the path my father watched impassively. I woke and remembered the dream, but could see no message in it.

I mentioned my dream jokingly a few days later to my stockbroker, John Delany, who said, "No, there *is* a message! I think it means you must stay where you are (trapped but unhurt), as the market *has already fallen*." Now several years later, it's clear that *to stay where I was* was excellent advice.

A friend, retired Bedford, Virginia, physician Bill McCabe, had a dream contact with his dead son Stuart Lynn McCabe on June 28, 1997, between five and six in the morning. I met the McCabes when I took a plant identification course at the Sedalia Center in Bedford, which is an old school that they bought and turned into a thriving community center. We became friends immediately, and have remained so since. He and his wife Annis agreed to let me publish it as he wrote it. Bill remarks in his cover letter that this was a "very vivid encounter" with the son they had lost about six years before, "much clearer and more real than usual dreams."

"Stuart appeared to me," Bill wrote, "in a military uniform with cap, resembling what were called 'dress-blues' as were seen when I was in the military. We seemed to be getting ready for something like a country fair—I was trying to get some animals (I believe cattle) ready for showing and was angry with Thom (another son) because he had not shown up to help me. Thom (Thomas McCabe) seemed younger than he is today, and his friends were there. When I asked them the whereabouts of Thom, suddenly Stuart appeared! He had blood on his face and uniform and one sleeve was torn open and blood oozing from an arm wound. He immediately came over and began to talk; told me he was just visiting for a short while and would soon be gone. After I hugged him and told him how glad I was to see him, I asked him quickly if he knew he had died, and he said 'Yes.' I then asked him how it felt to die, and he told me that the 'first five minutes are scary and that after that everything was fine.' He added that he was happy where he is now. I then (in the dream) ran to get Annis so that she could see him, and was afraid he would be gone when we returned but he was still there.

"At this point, we seemed to be at a public event and others would come up and try to talk to him, but he made no reply and seemed intent on only talking to us; he ignored the others. After I got Annis, she talked a lot to Stuart too. He told us we shouldn't be afraid to die. I asked him if we lived right could we expect to join him later and he quite casually assured me we would all be together again. He seemed glad to see us but appeared to be hurried…that he could not tarry long. We both told him how terribly we missed him and would have given gladly our own lives in his stead. He knew that, he said. I asked him if he ever visited either of his wives and he said he had seen Debbie but made no further elaboration. I asked him if he knew Doug Hardin had died, and he said he did and without any apparent emotion in the answer. We both talked to him and he seemed to have no problem in communicating with us and was obviously happy for the opportunity.

"He had obviously talked to Thom before he talked to us because Thom appeared about the time Stuart did. Stuart seemed to just want us all to know that he was fine where he was, that the 'other side' was 'no problem' and that dying and getting there was 'no problem.' Even though we were all hurried in our speech, Stuart did not seem to be grieving or hesitant over the fact that he had to go back or leave us. He gave the impression that he knew all that was going on in our lives since he left, when we tried to share those events with him.

"It seemed, however, that he was not aware of the time passed since his death and [thought] that it was natural or normal to visit us. He was calm about it all and reassuring that he was content and happy and really didn't feel that far from us, though he wasn't normally able to communicate with us.

"We embraced him several times and his body felt somewhat firm though not true 'rigor mortis.' Just before we last saw him, there seemed to be cattle around us to which he paid no attention. He then seemed to go into a room, and began to talk to us through a window. Suddenly he disappeared altogether.

"Annis and I were ecstatic over getting to see him and visit in the same old way as before death. He really tried to reassure us of his love and that 'everything was O. K.'

"I realized he was gone and awoke with tears in my eyes; we (Annis and I) were both crying with joy over having been able to see and talk to him once again."

A final note is that Annis, Bill's wife, asleep nearby, had no sense of being a part of the visit, nor did their son Thom. The dream was Bill's gift alone.

In the early 1950s, my friend Lisa Tracy of Lexington, recently retired from an editorial job with *The Philadelphia Inquirer*, had a dream about a girl she had met at camp named Bruce Norman, whom she had admired but not known well. Bruce was from a city about fifty miles away. Lisa was happily anticipating returning to Camp Lachlan, and hoped that Bruce Norman was also planning to return.

One night Lisa dreamed she went across Lexington and entered a house she knew while growing up, went up one set of stairs, and down some others onto a landing, where she found Bruce Norman in a wheelchair. Bruce said simply, in the dream, "I won't be coming back to camp this year."

Later, when Lisa got to camp, she learned that Bruce Norman had contracted rheumatic fever, was indeed in a wheelchair, and would not be coming back to camp. Lisa's dream image of Bruce in a wheelchair was an example of clairvoyance—seeing something clearly at a distance—with a probable mental telepathy between living minds, as Lisa's dreaming mind picked up from Bruce's mind the thought that Bruce wouldn't be coming to camp.

On October 11, 1999, the staid *New Yorker*, in reporting in "Annals of Disaster" on the vanished ship *Fantome*, reported, Early on the morning of the twenty-eighth, Captain Guyan's fiancee [Annie Bleasdale], who was in England, (the ship had just sunk in Belize) had an unsettling dream ... "that Guyan was with me in bed. He was dressed in white, and in the dream I knew that he wouldn't be there when I woke up, that this was goodbye." For several nights afterward, Bleasdale says that she awoke to find a hazy presence floating over her bed. Theosophists are familiar with this phenomenon; they describe it as an astral body. "I used to call him Angel," Bleasdale says. "The crew absolutely loved him."

In *Valley of the Golden Mummies*, (2000), Zahi Hawass, Director of Egypt's Supreme Council of the Antiquities, one of the world's most highly respected (and visible) archaeologists, recounts matter-of-factly a harrowing and remarkable haunting by the spirits of two mummified children whose grave he had uncovered.

After weeks of torment, he had a sudden *knowing* that the children needed to have their father with them. Once he returned to Egypt and moved the father's mummy to the museum where the children were, he was never again bothered by the terrifying nightly dream—wraiths of the frantic and angry children reaching to choke him, a claustrophobic sense of the children following him around crying and threatening—and a terrifying series of mishaps, missed flights, and near-accidents.

My father, I think, was not exactly *against* believing in the paranormal. He was just a hard-headed pragmatist. Aside from one strange predictive event in his over ninety years, he wasn't much interested in even thinking about things like that—but I was. There was never a time in my life when this one event didn't fascinate me, because if it was true it was enough to absolutely annihilate our linear concept of time, which has bothered me all my life since reading John Dunne's *Experiment in Time*.

This single psychic event occurred during my family's years in Peking (1936-1939) where my father was stationed, and where I was born in May 1938.

Daddy, a distinguished career Marine and tombstone General (meaning he was made General at retirement), dreamed one night that one of his soldiers was kicked to death by a horse down in the stables. The man's face was marked with a horse shoe print at a certain angle. As it was an extraordinarily clear, detailed dream, he recounted it during the bridge foursome he was part of later in the day, so that two other people along with my mother heard about the dream.

When the death actually occurred two days later, when the man was found dead exactly as in my father's dream, word got out that my father had known about this death ahead of the event, which led to an official investigation. My father was cleared of any involvement, because of his watertight alibi, but as with other supernatural events, the implications of such a dream are enormous. It has haunted me all my life that my rational father was not curious about this event. Whenever I'd pump him about it and ask what he thought had happened, he'd shrug, and say, "Coincidence, I guess."

I had a troubled relationship with my father, and five years after his death I was unaware of having had any dreams at all about him. Then one night in 1999 I dreamed that I was about to graduate from something, though it was unclear what. I had a great need to go get dressed appropriately so that I wouldn't be shabby or late for graduation. So I was in a hurry—as I often am in daytime life.

In the crowd cheering the graduates, *at some distance from me*, I saw my father. He was as I do not remember him: young, full of energy and fun, his hair golden and wavy shining in the sun, and he wore a turquoise blue short-sleeved T-shirt the same color as his eyes. He was laughing and supportive, cheering me on at my graduation.

In remembering it, the dream exactly characterized my hopes about my father. While he lived I wanted his approval more than I ever wanted anything else in my life, and now, finally, he seemed to be giving it. He was still at a distance, but he was approving—which suited me all right. I was still in a hurry. He was still distant. But he was *acknowledging* me, which I yearned for all my life.

Aunt Polly told me that when her father, my grandfather John Marston—also a career Marine—was stationed at the Naval Academy at Annapolis in the twenties, he sometimes walked to work through the nearby Naval Academy cemetery. One day he noticed his watch was missing, and he figured he'd lost it in the cemetery on his way to work. Although he retraced his steps and searched for it several times, he could never find it. He eventually bought a new watch and forgot about the old one.

Six months later he *dreamed* he was walking through the cemetery, where there was snow on the ground, and by a certain tombstone he saw a glint of gold in the snow. Reaching down, he found his lost watch. He told his family the dream in the morning, and said, "I think I'll just go through the cemetery and see." And it happened exactly as he'd dreamed it: there was the watch where he'd looked many times before—though oddly there was no snow.

An earring came back to me in a similar way. I lost one of my favorite 14-karat flat gold hoops one spring while morel-hunting. When I noticed it was missing, I had no idea where I could have lost it. I'd been in the woods with a friend, we'd gone to several of my favorite mushroom spots, and covered far too much ground for me to even think of going to look for it. I sent off the one earring I had left, and had another made just like it so I'd have a pair again.

About a year later, I woke in the night to recall something I'd certainly not remembered before—that when we'd parked and gotten out of the car at the town spring, I'd skinned off a sweater, as the day had gotten warm. *That's when I lost my earring*, I told myself. Just like that, out of the dead of night.

Next morning as soon as it was light, I drove to the town spring, and easily found the earring—bent and smashed into a muddy tire rut but still malleable, the gold still shiny. A year had passed, cars had been parked there, many feet had passed over the area, but there it was. I cleaned it up and coaxed it back into shape, and I've worn it ever since.

Mary Ellen Hagel, a voice coach and organist from Ann Arbor, Michigan, told me that many times in her life she has dreamed of being killed in a car wreck, dressed in clothes she thinks are from the twenties. In the dream, she is under an overpass, dead. She floats up to view the scene. Many details of the dream are clear. It occurs so frequently that she is convinced it happened—to the person she was in a past life. She was born in the thirties.

Adrienne Bodie of Lexington regales me for an hour at a New Year's day party with tales of her mother's psychic ability. Once, asleep after overeating, she had a clear dream of a dead aunt standing at the top of a long stair flight, beckoning to her to come with her, urging her up. Adrienne's mother was scared to go, and so did not. She woke up, gave a huge belch, and felt suddenly much better. She is convinced that if she had done her aunt's bidding and climbed the stairs, that she would have died.

Another time, Adrienne's mother was driving when she noticed ahead of her an old model car. She noticed that it turned off the road at some point. She thought nothing of it until she passed the place where she had seen it turn off—and there was no road of any sort there, and somehow the car had just vanished.

But Adrienne herself is psychic too. She saw her future husband, historian Charles Bodie, across a room, and instantly knew he was the man she would marry.

I dreamed early one morning, a month or so after the Garden Club ladies had come to visit, that under a bathroom cabinet were stowed three gallons of gin, on their sides, stacked atop one another. My husband was claiming that he'd stopped drinking, though he smelled boozy to me. I doubted my own perceptions because he swore he was not drinking, and I believed he'd never lied to me.

But I couldn't get that dream out of my head. When he went off for the day, I had to check, though I had never snooped before. I went directly to his bathroom cabinet, and there were the bottles exactly as I had seen them, only they were vodka. That's puzzling because I saw gin labels so clearly. Everything else was precisely what I dreamed. I have to conclude that some part of me had left my body and observed this scene.

6

Chances of Chance: Synchronicities

In 1952, Carl Gustav Jung wrote that coincidences occur much more frequently than probability theory would predict, thus undermining probability theory and suggesting a universal law we haven't discovered. He called these coincidences *synchronicity*: the phenomenon of apparently unrelated events occurring in a meaningful association with each other, and often in a string.

It was demonstrated by physicist John Bell in 1964 that two subatomic particles that have once been in contact, keep an attraction apparently forever, no matter how far apart. In fact, Jung tried to explain coincidences, telepathy, clairvoyance, and precognition all as manifestations of a single "acausal connecting principle" called synchronicity—which has "transcendent value" for those who experience the events—though the events themselves often seem trivial, even pointless. The trouble with Bell's theorem in a physical universe is that the subatomic particle attraction is instantaneous, even if the two particles are trillions of miles apart, and matter and energy as we know them cannot travel instantaneously. So Bell's theorem is a piece of the jigsaw puzzle of quantum physics that doesn't fit—yet. But of course you don't throw away a puzzle piece because it doesn't *appear* at the moment to fit in the puzzle you're working on.

It has been suggested that Bell's "attraction" does not involve energy, but the "influence of consciousness." According to an article in *Science Digest* (January 1982), physicist David Bohm posits that below the quantum level (which is below the atomic and sub-atomic levels) we will eventually find an even subtler sub-quantum level: a spaceless, timeless realm—in which all things turn out to be part of everything else—that causes ordinary reality and, can also cause extraordinary reality such as synchronicities. And thus we arrive back at Buddhism, ancient Greek thought, and other mystical conclusions that *All is One*. If indeed that is the nature of reality, it makes sense that we can occasionally by accident, or by intention, by learning how, contact another part of the realm that is us, each of us, all of all of us.

What looks to be happening is some attraction, some *new gravity* that, instead of pulling us down onto the earth, exists between items and people in a way that *has* meaning, even if we don't understand it. Many synchronicities are minor and even apparently silly, but some are truly striking.

David Chalmers in 1995 published an article in *Scientific American* in which he put forth the theory that consciousness is as real as matter or energy; he declares there's plenty of evidence that it's not made by the brain nor dependent on the brain for its reality. This is possibly why prayer heals, why people experience ghosts, why synchronicities occur, and why we can "know" things we shouldn't be able to know on occasion.

A story of mine, "Rainbow," is included in an anthology of American short stories, a National Public Radio project, called *I Thought My Father Was God*. Reading my way through the collection slowly, I was astonished at how many of the short stories in the anthology are about amazing synchronicities—or coincidences—*far more than on any other theme*. Following are some more significant synchronicities.

In the April 2002 Johns Hopkins *Alumni Review*, a story is told about Tom Cirillo, a 1976 Arts and Science graduate.

"In September 1990, Cirillo was in California training to go to the Persian Gulf when a helicopter from a neighboring squadron" went down in the ocean nearby, losing the entire crew. Later, "it became Cirillo's job to lead the mission to recover the helicopter."

While surveying the wreckage, Cirillo noticed a pilot's helmet on the sea floor, but did not stop to recover it. Three years later, Cirillo, by then the commanding officer of the squadron to which the downed helicopter had belonged, received a call that a fishing trawler had netted a helmet belonging to Tim Hanusin, the co-pilot of the crashed helicopter. Cirillo, realizing the family had never had a body to bury, thought they might value especially Tim's helmet.

Cirillo decided to make the presentation himself. When he did, he learned that Hanusin's mother, named Rosemarie, had recently died after a long illness, having "told her children that she would do her best to give them a sign that she and Tim were together in heaven." Hanusin's helmet had been recovered on Tim's birthday, and the children all believed that this was the sign they'd been waiting for—especially since the name of the boat that netted the helmet was *Rosemarie*.

Cirillo now believes "that there are no circumstances that occur on their own—there is a grand design."

David McKnight's brother, John (Jack) McKnight, from Evanston, Illinois, related through David how he was recently serendipitously reunited with a college classmate, one Joe Farruggia, whom Jack had not seen since college graduation, and of whose whereabouts he had no clue.

One Monday morning, Jack flew from Chicago to speak at a conference held in Eureka, California.

That morning, Joe Farruggia *happened to be wondering* what his old friend Jack McKnight had been doing through the years, and decided to call Northwestern University, their mutual *alma mater*, to see if the school had any record of John McKnight's current address. Joe was completely unaware that Jack was a professor at Northwestern. The school operator switched the call to Jack's department, where the secretary told Joe that Jack was away at a conference, but that she would give him a message about the call.

Before ending the call, she asked Joe where he was calling from, and he said, "Oh, it doesn't matter; just give him the message, please."

But for some reason the secretary persisted, and Joe said, "I'm calling from California."

The secretary responded, "Well, Mr. McKnight is in Eureka, California, this week for a conference."

Joe Farrugia replied, "I'm retired, and living ten miles from Eureka." The secretary said she would give Joe's telephone number to Jack when they talked later that day. By evening, Jack was on the phone with Joe, and they had dinner together the next day—having been completely out of touch with each other for 47 years!

On September 10, 2000, the *Roanoke Times* reported the story of a surveyor, John Langlois, who found a purse in bad condition in a patch of woods behind a school near Norfolk, Virginia. Full of insurance papers and other documents which told the story of its owner, one Sally Wallis, it was easy to find the owner.

Sally had lost it in a purse-snatching fifteen months before. The purse contained $2500, and her entire life's worth of information, which she always by habit carried with her.

Since the theft Sally had changed all the locks in the house, and all the bank numbers and credit-card numbers. But she was never free of the fear that the thief knew too much about her and might come after her.

Then, adding to her mental burden, her husband sickened, then died, leaving her alone—her greatest terror. Before the funeral she and her son sat at the kitchen table and prayed that she would be safe now that she was alone, that somehow, someday, she'd get her purse back, and they asked God to send them a sign.

As she walked into her house *right after the funeral* the phone rang with the news that her purse had been found, only the few dollars in her wallet missing—the $2500 in cash still rested in an envelope undetected in the bottom of the purse, and all the papers, though moldy and full of insects, were intact.

She believed her prayers had been answered, and that Langlois and the school secretary who called her were "angels." Her conclusion: "You have to believe that's truly a miracle."

I am sitting with my friend and long-time mentor/angel Adelaide Simpson on her side porch, sipping iced tea made the way it ought to be, with fresh stems of mint and real sugar and transparent slices of lemon floating in clear amber. It's an official condolence visit, though I am late, her husband having been dead several months. The heavy scent of her world-class roses fills the air. She is wearing on her collar a pin made of x's and o's that looks like real diamonds and gold. She always signs letters and notes with a series of x's ad o's, kisses and hugs, so I comment on how appropriate her pin seems.

She brightens. Her husband, Herbie, who died just weeks before their fiftieth anniversary, had always been a terrible present-giver, she reports, presenting her with a bathrobe with a red dragon slithering down the back, or horrible gold and purple earrings that reminded her of a gypsy. So, soon after they were married, she'd taken to turning down the pages of catalogues and marking things she wanted and putting them on Herbie's desk, thus ending up with the presents she fancied.

The XXXOOO sign-off has always been her personal signature. So when she saw an XXXOOO pin in the Tiffany catalogue soon after Herbie's death, she fell in love with it. Still suffering the raw sorrow of her bereavement, she decided to treat herself to an anniversary present from Herbie. So she called them, and ordered the pin. She wanted it to arrive in time for the anniversary—even though Herbie had missed it.

Sorry, they said, it would take longer than that. She explained that it was important to her to have it right away, told them her husband had just died, their anniversary was coming up.

Tiffany's graciously agreed to do their best to speed the process, and the pin, as beautiful as it had appeared in the catalogue, arrived just two days later, on their anniversary. She put it on that day, and has worn it ever since.

Weeks later, it crossed her mind that she'd never been billed. So she called Tiffany's, and they said that the pin had been paid for. She assured them it had not been. But they checked again, and stated that her account was fully paid.

Who could have paid for it? The store? But that would have included a letter, some acknowledgement of her loss, some indication that the gift was on the house. The store denied that that was the case, insisting that the bill had been paid.

Could she have mentioned ordering it to her son who lives in New York, leading him to secretly pay for it? But her son replied that if he'd spent five hundred dollars on a present, he'd sure take credit for it.

There simply wasn't anyone else who could or would have paid for it; in fact—she'd told no one else about it. To this day, she has no idea who paid for her elegant Kisses and Hugs pin—but is sure it has to have been Herbie somehow, from another realm, where perhaps anything is possible.

Coincidence or synchronicity? From 1963 until 1987 I taught English at Southern Seminary Junior College, a women's school in Buena Vista, now Southern Virginia University. Each faculty member was asked to host a student-faculty tea once a year. The dining room provided tea. Some teachers or staff would bake cookies, some would buy doughnuts. One year, for a lark, I announced that for my tea, there would be a "world-famous" tea-reading fortune teller.

For the occasion I asked the kitchen staff to provide us with un-bagged tea in the pots. I read a book on how to read tea leaves, donned a curly black wig (I am a straight-haired blonde), and the students lined up to have their fortunes told. I "read" their leaves, telling them how soon they would marry, making merry stories about how many children they would have, whether their futures were serene or hectic, and other silly matters. There were some shapes of tea leaves that, according to the book I had read, symbolized love, wealth, success, sickness, and so on; and when those appeared I pointed them out.

Understand that I was doing this in a spirit of pure fun, thinking the students would find the wig absurd and funny. I was relaxed, and there was much awe, laughter, and confirmation: "Four children? All my life I've wanted four children!" or, "You say I'm going to marry a military man? Well, I'm engaged to a Marine!" or, "An archaeologist? How did you know that's my dream?"

Giddy with success (we had over 300 students at the college, and most of them seemed to want their fortunes read), I was scooting along interpreting the "symbols" stuck inside their cups, when suddenly I saw the distinct shape of a gun on the side of a girl's cup. Without thinking—I was still in the joking mode—I said, "Oh, there's a gun here."

The girl's hands flew to her face, and she shrieked—pretty much breaking up the tea party. Her father had shot himself to death a month before. I was so unnerved that I never read tea leaves again. I don't know how many of my predictions came true, of course. I had only been *playing*, unself-consciously allowing the symbols to bubble to the surface. Some part of my higher self, I have to think, led me in this method, which didn't involve conscious analysis, or even trying. I was just playing. I still recall the awed responses over and over, that I'd hit the nail on the head.

On Sept. 6, 1881, a Virginia Military Institute cadet named James Harvey Maxwell drowned in the north branch of the James, now called the Maury River, that runs by VMI. Subsequently, his sister established a scholarship for a needy cadet in James Maxwell's memory. Nearly a century later, on July 29, 1969, Larry Howard Foster, a VMI cadet, the current recipient of the James Maxwell Scholarship, drowned in the same stretch of river that had killed his benefactor.

Rader Dod, whom I grew up with in Lexington, Virginia, was in his boat in Florida on the inland waterway, looking for a place to dock and spend the night. At dusk, as he was cruising, looking for a space to tie up the boat, a lady on a dock looked up, and said, "Aren't you Rader Dod?"

"Yes," he replied. "Who the hell are you?"

She replied with her name, and said, "I dated you in college."

Rader and his wife Ellie went ashore and stayed with her two days. (Their daughter Bryan Dod Mines told me this story.)

While pregnant with our second child in 1977, I *happened* to be a part of a team of five writers for a public television series called *Footsteps*, and I *happened* to be assigned to write a story on *parental reactions to discovering that they have a handicapped child*. According to the limited literature I could drum up in those days before computers, even before databases, the reactions of parents—upon discovering that their child is somehow damaged—are much the same as the grief reactions Elizabeth Kubler-Ross had listed only a couple of years before: *denial, anger, bargaining, depression,* and *acceptance*. I wrote down that list, thought about it, devised scenes showing all of those stages for the little country family I'd invented, who learn, early in his life, that their infant son Teddy is deaf.

And so I wrote the script "I'll Dance at Your Wedding" for the PBS *Footsteps Series*, never thinking for an instant that the benefits of the exercise would be any more than the fee I was paid. I would later observe myself going through all the stages of my grief, though not necessarily in any order. This seeming "chance" assignment of the subject gave me much-needed stability when, five months later, I gave birth to a handicapped daughter. When our baby was born, because of what I had been studying, I was able to step back from my grief and confusion, get hold of myself, review my research, and learn from the reactions of other parents who'd experienced similar things. What a gift from the universe! Today it strikes me as impossible that that was just some incredible coincidence. I have written more about that experience is my memoir about my daughter: *ALL TIME IS NOW: Adventures with Jennie*.

September 1, 1997: on the day I happen to be *talking about synchronicity* to an Elderhostel class I am teaching, my friend Marysue Forrest calls from our local bookstore, The Bookery, to tell me that the oddest thing has happened!

First, in July, just before my memoir, *When The Fighting Is All Over*, came out, I'd done a reading from the forthcoming book at a Richmond women's club, during which it occurred to me I should strike while the iron was hot. If I didn't sell the books in advance, on that day, the women, no matter how enthusiastic, no matter how good-intentioned, no matter how crazy about the book, would forget to buy it in three months when it actually appeared in bookstores.

Thus I suggested at the end of my talk that anyone who wanted a signed copy of the book when it came from the publisher should sign up on a tablet at the door, and I'd arrange to send the autographed books, with a bill enclosed, from one of our local bookstores. Forty-seven people signed up to buy the book, and nineteen others wrote letters later to reserve copies.

When the book finally arrived, Marysue filled the orders as we had agreed, putting the letters in the books so that I could personalize my autographs. I went down to The Bookery, wrote in all the books, and collected the letters.

What has happened, Marysue now explains, is that I had left one of the letters in one of the books I'd signed that she was going to send to the Richmond women. My conscious intent had been to bring the letters home and file them—and I thought I had done so.

But Marysue was excited because—the letter I accidently left in a book I'd signed was from a woman named Cindy Smith that *Marysue used to be best friends with, back in Texas*, had lost track of—and now can correspond with again.

So an unconscious, or perhaps superconscious, intent had overridden the conscious one. Had I not *accidently* left the letter in the book, she'd not have read it. Details of the letter made her realize it was not some other of a zillion Cindy Smiths, but her friend Cindy Smith, now living in Richmond. Had I, she wants to know, somehow *known* that and left the letter there on purpose? Of course I had not. Not consciously, anyway.

When we bought Wilson Springs farm near Goshen Pass in western Rockbridge County, and my (now-ex) husband traced the deed back to the Borden Grant by King George III of England in the 1730s, he discovered that the original grant had been made to *a direct ancestor of his, Daniel Strickler*. I should add that we knew nothing of the farm's history before we acquired it. I was struck with amazement at the coincidence. But my ex-husband, always skeptical, said, "There are thirty thousand people in Rockbridge County, and if you traced back to 1736 you'd probably have 30,000 ancestors. It doesn't seem all that remarkable to me." And there you have it, our two views.

Louisa Rhine, wife of the famous Duke parapsychologist, and herself a noted parapsychologist, once wrote, "Almost every tentative psi experience could be interpreted as a coincidence." Thus each of us creates our own version of reality, based on our beliefs.

Mary and David McKnight were coming for the weekend, and we had no plans except dinner and an evening of conversation. We had a house near us we planned to visit the next morning, to try to communicate with the spirits that seemed to be haunting it.

All summer, a couple of actors from the Lime Kiln Theater outside Lexington had attended my aerobics class. I went to all the new productions, but had no plans to go to see Lime Kiln's set-piece, "Stonewall Country," which I've seen probably thirty times in its seventeen-year history. I even helped to edit it back when it was being written.

But a sassy boy named Jack kept telling me I had to come: it was different, and better, this year, he insisted. He was playing J.E.B. Stuart. He and I enjoyed a silly flirtation: I was completely safe, being married, over sixty, and by far the eldest member of the aerobic dance class. He was at most eighteen.

It occurred to me that maybe David and Mary would like to see "Stonewall Country," and closing night was when they were coming to stay over. So I asked if they would like to go, and they were delighted, having never seen the show, so I called the theater the day before the show closed. I explained I needed four tickets near the front, as I am hard of hearing and even with hearing aids have to lip-read a lot.

The reservations girl said that was impossible, that they were nearly sold out, and any tickets left would be way in the back, and probably not even together.

I hesitated—then it occurred to me that I already knew the play so well I didn't *need* to hear. I was just saying what I say whenever I make theater reservations. So, letting go of any attachment at all, I said, "Okay, anywhere is fine, then."

And I swear this happened: at that instant, the girl at the desk said, "Oh, my goodness. We've just had a cancellation for four tickets in the middle of the front row."

We went, David and Mary amazed at the perfect seats I'd gotten on such short notice (me, too!). Near the end of the show, my young beau Jack came leaping offstage in a dance number, grabbed me from my seat, and dragged me up on stage to dance with him. If it had been any other than closing night, I presume such silliness could have gotten him fired. I was flabbergasted, and when I returned to my seat, stumbling and blinded by the stage lights, David leaned over and said to me, "And you think you never have paranormal experiences?"

Once, on a hike with VMI professor Tom Greet, a friend of ours now dead, we sat on the ground resting and *talking about possible Indian habitation of our cliff-above-river position*. Tom reached back to lean on his hands. One of his hands landed on something sharp. It was a *perfect* Indian projectile point in the muddy grass, the only undamaged one we had ever found. What a coincidence! Or was it synchronicity?

Reading *The Holographic Universe* by Michael Talbot some years ago, I had just read the section on synchronicity, and about how the name "Buffalo Bill" kept coming up for him. I had gone into the kitchen to make a cup of coffee, book still in my hand. My husband came in clutching the paper, talking about the Super Bowl, and remarking that our stock in Tultex was doing well because they're the ones who make the Washington Redskins shirts, and that zillions of them had sold. "Who're the Redskins playing?" I asked, being sports-challenged in the extreme, but trying to be polite.

"The Buffalo Bills," he replied.

Recently a friend who lives way out of town and doesn't have much money asked me, when I was going to spend the day with him, to go to CVS Pharmacy and bring him some Vitamin E capsules. I said I'd bring them as a gift, but he would have none of it. "Oh, no, I insist on paying for them." The CVS pharmacy didn't open for *ten more minutes* when I got there, so I decided I'd go across the street to Kroger and get some things I needed, then return to CVS. At Kroger, with the Vitamin E on my mind, I wondered if they might have some. Indeed they did, a two-for-one special on certain vitamins. The Vitamin E was nearly twelve dollars, and so I was able to get one for myself at that cost—and tell my friend quite honestly that *his* had been absolutely free!

At my Elderhostel course in September 1999, I'm having lunch with some of the participants, totally at random as I always do, and one man—whose body language has already told me he's depressed—tells me, when I ask what he does, that he's just retired.

"Retired from what?" I ask.

"*The Baltimore Sun*," he says.

Because a girl I didn't remember in high school, Lydia S., who showed up at the reunion for all classes of our small high school the week before, had told me she works for *The Baltimore Sun*, I am prompted to ask, "Oh, do you know Lydia S.?"

I'm thinking of Lydia S. because I'd been asked to sign books at the reunion, and she'd bought two of my books and stood around awhile chatting. As we talked, she'd seemed sad, describing a recent failed love affair.

The man seated next to me goes absolutely pale at my mention of Lydia S., glances nervously over at his wife, then says, in a strained, muted manner, "Of course. Everyone there knows everyone else. She's a sweet girl." His wife is talking to someone on the other side of her, and seems not to notice. But he's a nervous wreck, his composure shattered. He can't finish lunch.

Somehow, I know what will happen, and it does. He waylays me later alone in the hall as I am already sure he will do, and asked rather nervously, *How do you know Lydia?*

And of course I have to play dumb, so I just say casually oh, that we just knew each other slightly in high school—but it's clear to me that *he* is the lover she'd just told me about breaking up with.

I teach ten or twelve Elderhostel classes every year for Virginia Commonwealth University, with forty to fifty people in each one. To think of all the events that had to line up to culminate in that chance meeting, that chance inquiry, among all the people who come from all over the United States to our Elderhostels!

When I bought a set of Emergency Healing tapes for my friend Jane Merrill, due to go in January of 1992 for a bone-marrow transplant for multiple myeloma, I also thought vaguely that I'd like to include a Metamusic tape for her. Then I forgot about it. I ordered some other tapes for myself, including one called "Eddys." (The Emergency Healing Tapes and Metamusic Tapes are copyrighted products of the Monroe Institute in Faber, Virginia.)

When I got home with my bag of tapes, I found I had two "Eddys" tapes, my favorite of the music tapes I'd heard that TMI puts out. I then searched to see what tape might have been omitted from my order, which had included one "Eddys"—but nothing was missing, there was just an extra "Eddys," as if the universe had complied with my desire to give Jane a tape that could perhaps relax her towards her passage out of this life.

Throughout her last sad year, Jane, in increasing pain as her bone cancer progressed, complained about the mail box at the tiny Rockbridge Baths Post Office because it happened to be turned around the wrong way, the mail slot facing away from the road, so that she (and everyone else) had to stop, get out of the car, walk around to the *back* where the slot was, to mail letters. Moving was extremely painful for her.

She always said she was going to complain to the post office, and get them to fix it. Maybe she did; I don't know.

The *morning of the day after Jane's death*, in the late summer of 1997, when Jane's close friend Mame Warren drove to town, Mame suddenly noticed that the mail box was turned around the right way, so that you could mail a letter without getting out of the car. Amazed, she went in to ask the postmistress about it.

"Oh, I've bugged them *forever* to come fix it, and the guy just showed up yesterday morning and did it," the woman replied. Mame, struck by the perfect timing, feels that Jane somehow managed to influence the reversing of the annoying mail box that had irked her for so long. To others, it might look like coincidence.

Paul Shue was my friend, companion, and research assistant during my writing of *Scalded to Death By the Steam*, and *The Man Who Wanted Seven Wives*. I met him in 1982 and we were friends until his death in 1987.

In 1991, when I was writing an article about ginseng, I was referred to the president of the Wisconsin ginseng association, a Taiwanese named *Paul Hsu* who was greatly helpful to me, though we never met in person. Their names are pronounced exactly the same.

There is a phenomenon I've come to call *Lyle's Law of Duality*—but you have undoubtedly experienced it, too. My ex-husband and I share(d) an interest in new words and word origins, and we have long noticed that a day or so after we've come across a new word, it appears again. It happens with facts, too; someone talks about the high tide in the bay of Fundy, and before a day is out, someone else unrelated to the original conversation will mention it, or you'll open a magazine at random, and there before your eyes is an article about the Bay of Fundy.

Lyle's Law goes: *a new thing will occur or be mentioned again in a short time*. It's a form of synchronicity, and it happens all the time. The following story is an excellent example.

The phone rings on a Sunday morning while we're having breakfast. Dan Morrow, the voice identifies itself; interested in a murder that occurred in Lexington in 1854. Someone has referred him to us. This happens fairly regularly, as we are both writers, and have interest in many subjects, including local history.

I write down the name while it's still ringing in my ear, and turn the phone over to my husband, because it's not a subject I'm familiar with.

I recall vaguely that the guy said he was from somewhere I've heard of: oh, yes,—Waterford. That's the crystal. End of conversation.

When my husband hangs up a few minutes later, having told the fellow he's heard of the murder but doesn't know anything about it, I am putting dishes in the washer. My husband remarks, "He was looking for information on an 1854 murder of a VMI cadet."

Normally, I wouldn't have gotten that much information, for we don't necessarily report to each other on all the inquiries we get, some relevant to our areas of interest, some not.

I go back to my office to work some more on a current project involving my grandparents' letters and papers. For some reason, as I thumb through some files, the date 1854 catches my eye. Curious, I pull it, see it is a thick handwritten document of maybe seventy pages, and after scanning only a few lines, I realize that it is *a long deposition, or more than one, on the case the caller was asking about.*

Only because I wrote his name down, and recalled Waterford crystal, was I able to retrieve his name from the trash can, find a number, call him up, and leave a message that, astonishingly, I'd stumbled onto material on the thing he was looking for, only a few moments after our conversation. He was at our house within hours.

When I was leaving for Honduras hastily in the summer of 1998 to help with a dig, hours before I left I found open in the bathroom a *National Geographic*, turned to an article about Copan, which I knew was one of the places I would visit. I was enchanted that the new magazine had an article about exactly where I was going, stuck it in my bag, and read it on the plane to Honduras.

Arriving, I breathlessly tried to share it with my fellow volunteers, only to discover that the article (and the *National Geo*) was six years old! What I never could figure out was (1) why hadn't I seen it before, since the Mayans are one of my passions, and (2) how did it come to be in the bathroom open to that article the day I was leaving? My husband was the only person who could have pulled that off, and he swore he had nothing to do with it, had never seen it!

The following story happened at Otis Mead's grandmother's funeral. Between the funeral service and the burial in the cemetery, Otis needed to entertain his children, then about six and eight. So he took them around to see family burial markers. He paused at his father's grave (who had died young), and saw that the stone read: *Aged 40 years, 3 mos and 5 days.*

Since he was forty at the time, Otis got to figuring. First he realized he was about three months into his fortieth year. Then—he figured out that he was, on that day, *the same age his father had been when he died.* How amazing that he should find himself standing at that spot on that day. When he pointed out this remarkable coincidence to his wife Sue Ann, she said drily, raising an eyebrow, "Just be careful driving home."

Otis Mead's now-deceased wife, Sue Ann, one day took a package to the local Pack 'n Mail store. While she was waiting in line, the phone rang. The man behind the counter answered it, looked up, said, "Anyone here named Mrs. Mead?" She'd never been in the store before. She'd told nobody she was going there, and it was only one among several errands she had to go on that day.

She took the call, puzzled as to how anyone could have found her there. It was nothing significant, just a furrier phoning her from Roanoke about a coat she was buying or storing, and the man *thought* he'd called her home number, which ends in 2740. The Pack 'n Mail number has the same prefix, and ends in 7740. Only one digit off, an understandable and minor error.

But is it not *strange* that she should have been at that exact moment at the place the furrier managed by accident to call?

December of 1996, the local Episcopal minister David Cox called and asked for my then-husband one morning about eight. Now I'm lapsed Episcopalian, and he is, in his own words, a recovering Presbyterian, so I was curious about why the local Episcopal minister wanted my Presbyterian husband. So later I asked him. He told me that the R.E. Lee Memorial Episcopal Church was uncovering some murals, and David had called him to come down and photograph them and maybe offer some advice on what to do. My husband is locally famous as the author of *The Architecture of Historic Lexington*, a brisk seller ever since the University Press of Virginia published it in 1977.

But as things transpired, my husband was busy; and so I said I'd go down and photograph the murals, as I was heading for the VMI rare book room and records to check out some files about my family, and the church was right on my way. So I photographed the murals about 1:00 that day, and went on to my research at the VMI library.

And in my great-uncle John D. Letcher's file, about 3:00, I came across a 1931 letter advising against covering up some murals in the Episcopal church. JDL had written the letter to the vestry, a copy of which was still in his file. The letter included the warning, "*History will judge you harshly if you remove or destroy them.*"

Amused at the coincidence, I made a Xerox of my great-uncle's letter and took it by to David Cox. Next Sunday, he quoted the letter from the pulpit, and the result was a decision to halt the destruction of the murals. *A voice from the past told them to.* I need to report that, as things eventually turned out, they destroyed most of the murals anyway, preserving only a small part of them around the chancel. Perhaps history's "harsh judgment" is still in the future.

The obnoxious woman in her church congregation was making my friend LuAnne Patrick miserable, and Lu prayed about it long and hard: how could she love this petty, jealous person who made snide remarks, refused to speak to her, spread gossip around like mayonnaise? One Sunday, leaving church after an especially difficult confrontation with the woman, LuAnne raised her eyes to Heaven, and said in exasperation, out loud, "*Oh, God, just let me fix her little red wagon!*"

It snowed all day, and that night after the church supper, cars were having a hard time of it getting out of the parking lot. Traffic moved slowly, then the car in front of Lu's wouldn't start. She sent her oldest son to give the car a push, but it wasn't the slick hill: the car's engine had stalled. Then Lu climbed out, and thought she might try something her husband had shown her a few days before when her car had stalled. She tapped on the window—and saw too late it was her nemesis. But now she had to help. "Flip your hood open," Lu said. "I think it's the butterfly valve."

With a deft motion, Lu unscrewed the top of the air filter, found and lifted the valve. It was the one auto repair in the world she knew how to do.

The car started easily, the woman offered a rather faint-hearted thank you. As the woman drove off, passing under a streetlight, Lu noticed coincidentally that she was driving a *dark red station wagon*.

Oh, God, just let me fix her little red wagon!

What are the chances of that happening?

I venture the observation that these true events seem to point to a compelling force in the universe, far beyond human understanding. We are offered glimpses of meaning in the midst of so many apparently meaningless events that surround us all the time. Perhaps they are signs that can lead us to faith.

7

Gifts from the Other Side: Apports

My childhood friend Jeanne Tracy Eichelburger—told me this story that happened to her and a friend of hers in Binghamton, New York, where she now lives, and is Head of Special Collections, University Archives and Preservation for SUNY at Binghamton.

Susie Conole lived her entire life in the house where she was born, along with her two brothers, all three continuing to live there after their parents died. Susie herself died soon after the events in this story happened.

The siblings were all beset by multiple health problems; none ever married; all lived at home; and there was not much money to go around. In 1994, the oldest brother, Paul, died of liver failure. A month later, the second brother, Phil, died, leaving sister Susie alone in the house they'd all grown up in. Now everything belonged to her.

Exhausted and grieving, and ill herself, Susie invited Jeanne to go to Alaska with her on a cruise, as a nurse-companion, with Jeanne's fare fully paid. As vacations do, the trip ended up being more expensive than Susie had planned, and one day she was fretting aloud about running out of money before the trip was over. Jeanne could not help, as she was on a tight budget herself, and could not have afforded the money to go on the trip.

One day Susie announced to Jeanne, "There's a man on this trip that looks like Phil (her dead brother). Look!"

Jeanne had known Phil, and stared to where Susie, in a wheelchair, pointed to a man some distance away with his back to them. "My God," Jeanne agreed, "he really does."

Jeanne tried to move to a place where she could see the man's face better, but could not, as a crowd of people on deck who had been watching something in the water began at that point to move inside for lunch, forcing Jeanne to maneuver Susie's wheelchair. In the jostle Jeanne couldn't find the man again.

At lunch they continued to discuss the striking resemblance, and they vowed to continue looking for the stranger, since they were to be on the ship for several more days.

There were two odd outcomes. The first was that, though there were only about 150 people on the ship, neither woman ever saw again the man who looked so like Phil.

The second was that Susie, in some alarm at her rapidly shrinking funds, went through her purse again later on the day they had spotted the lookalike—and found five hundred dollars tucked away that she was absolutely certain had not been there earlier.

Afterwards Susie believed her brother's appearance, witnessed by her and Jeanne both, had somehow been a sign that he was still looking after her materially as well as spiritually—and that it was the deceased Phil who had, in the form of an angel, managed to ease Susie's financial worries.

Many people, I have discovered, have received physical gifts from the dead, which have a name: apports.

Mama must have forgotten about her near-death experience in Peking, for she and I talked about paranormal things in her last days quite often, and she was agnostic if not atheist, generally convinced that death was the finality. She'd had an unhappy relationship with my father, and once or twice wondered sadly if anything other than oblivion would follow life, but by then was so sick she didn't much care. I had no beliefs myself then about an Afterlife, but I made her promise that if it turned out that we were wrong in believing that you just died, period, that she would find a way to let me know.

After Mama's death, I tried to be "open" and listen. I ran every night, all over town, and always in the cemetery, which is right down the street from where I live. I visited her grave and put flowers on it. I talked to her, though it seemed clear to me she wasn't there. Summer faded, winter came and went, and it was in the spring (because I'd just put a jar of daffodils down at the grave) when I saw the little blue butterfly. I think it's called a "Blue." It flew up in front of me, seeming to just come right out of the ground. I remember that happening, but I attached no significance to it.

At home I looked and looked for signs, but never perceived anything—of course I had no concept of what I was looking for. Yet about nine months after her death, I was hunting morels in the spring woods when a dark blue Diana butterfly paced me, stayed with me, would perch on a low branch just ahead of where I paused. It would wait for me to move on. When it flew it conveyed quite clearly the message, HAPPY HAPPY HAPPY! It seemed odd behavior for a butterfly (though what else do butterflies do?) and, for some reason, after a bit I perceived it was Mama.

My ex-husband is an amateur naturalist, and as I told him later that day about my attentive butterfly visitor on the mountain, another blue Diana came and flittered across the terrace right in front of us. We laughed at the "coincidence," and I commented that the one that had followed me was bigger than the one on our terrace. "The females are bigger," he said.

Though at the time of her death in 1979 I had no spiritual belief at all, and therefore felt I was being crazy to think so—a result of missing her—I continued to "perceive" that Mama was visiting me in the form of those butterflies that would seem to check in with me from time to time, always seeming to convey the same joyful message, HAPPY HAPPY HAPPY! I have written about my growing perception of this in my 1998 memoir *When the Fighting is All Over* (Atlanta, Longstreet).

There's a postscript to this story: My sister Betsy Letcher Greenlee, who is very skeptical, admits this occurrence made her shiver. She was politely amused by my stories of Mama and the butterflies, but could not buy it as truth.

In 1993, she and I went on a trip to London together. It was a research venture for me, and she tagged along. Because I like going to the SAGB (the Spiritual Association of Great Britain) for readings, I bought her a half-hour session with a psychic, and more or less forced her to go. As she had some issues with our mother when she was young, she was apparently talking to the psychic about this, when the psychic interrupted her to say, "Why do I feel that a butterfly just came into this room?" The psychic knew nothing of my idyll about our mother, and nothing about either one of us. Betsy told me that it made the hair stand up on the back of her neck.

Doubters will say we are only *selectively noticing* repeated common events. It is the second notice of something that "sets us up." We noticed the attention of a butterfly *like that one we saw yesterday,* or we may hear a familiar song a second time that reminds us of a person we've lost. Then we hear the same song or see that butterfly a *third* time. Okay, it could still be coincidence, of course. But what made me notice the butterflies only after my mother died?

And now I learn that the butterfly, transforming as it does from a creeping insect into a beautiful flying creature, is a symbol for the soul in many cultures. Probably I already knew that, but I sure didn't connect it with Mama.

Sometimes objects with special meaning seem almost to materialize on our paths, as if they were gifts from loved ones who are no longer with us. When I admitted almost jokingly (well, it was *embarrassing!*) to some friends my perceptions about my mother, I learned that some of them have had similar experiences. I can't possibly say why suddenly a *certain* passing butterfly will strike me as being my mother—but it does. Not all butterflies by any means; just occasionally, and it's always so *obvious*! I've rationalized it by saying that Mama, an artist, loved bright colors and changed clothes often, and collected butterflies during her later years. But it is amazing when they show up, and I have what feels like a "knowing" that it is my mother checking up on how I'm doing. It's a physical being that calls my long-dead mother to mind. From her perspective, maybe it's a way of letting me know she's connected with me still.

Friend Jacqui Simanek calls from Mount Pleasant, South Carolina. Her cousin Nell had died. They did a lot of things together, including cooking and exchanging recipes. Soon after Nell died, Jacqui needed a fig jam recipe. She knew she had one *somewhere* but could not find it, even after several days of searching.

Next morning when she walked out on her porch, there lying on the floor, was a recipe for fig jam. It was not in her handwriting. Jacqui's family used the porch all the time; nobody had spied the 3 x 5 handwritten card there the day before, or ever. Did it fall out of one of the books Jacqui had been sifting through? Though an ordinary (though coincidental!) explanation is certainly possible, perhaps even likely, Jacqui thinks that cousin Nell managed somehow, from beyond the grave, to get her the recipe she was looking for.

My old friend Tut believes that she received gifts of white feathers from her first husband, Minor, for a time after he died. It happened to her exactly as it did to me: at some point it just crossed her mind that the white feathers she kept coming across, or that seemed so frequently to just drift down in front of her on the sidewalk, were gifts from Minor, just to say he was still there, or here, or with her in vibration. The point seemed to be, he was *not dead* if he could still send her gifts. Again, an object with a history of spiritual significance: soul is light as a feather; angels have wings, which are made of feathers…

After my mushroom-hunting buddy Burwell Wingfield's mother died, he began to find her hairpins here and there. He says it happened for *years* after all her things had been removed from the house and the house had been vacuumed hundreds of times. There, on the floor behind the bathroom sink, there, in the middle of the hall carpet, would appear one of her hairpins. Burwell took it that she was keeping in touch.

An old ex-beau of mine, Sam Syme, still comes to visit when he's in town for a Washington and Lee alumni event. He says that, since his mother's death, he's found pennies that he believes she's left for him.

When I asked why he thought the pennies were from her, he said the first one appeared one morning soon after her death on a dresser where her picture was. There lay a penny, where he was sure none had been the night before. When Sam examined it, he discovered that it was an Indian head penny from 1899, the year of his mother's birth.

Since then, finding pennies in odd places, he feels they come from her, just letting him know she is still "here" in some sense, still looking after him. An apparent further confirmation: both of his children have come across pennies and come to the same conclusion as he has, all three of them more or less independently of each other.

I even found a *negative* apport story, actually two: in the seventies Barbara Wassell (now Goldsten) and her family rented a 21-room house on Long Island, built in 1727, near where her husband was stationed. Barbara got interested in hearth cooking while living there, and taught classes in it that culminated in a whole meal cooked on the ancient hearth.

One time she had seven youngsters in the class, and among other things they were cooking baked apples on the hearth. Every child prepared one apple, and Barbara set them up in a Dutch oven, six around, one in the middle, and put them to cook in the hot coals—with more coals heaped over the top—for their dessert. She says she and everyone else were in the room the entire time.

When the Dutch oven was opened, there were only six apples. No one had touched the pan, which had been heaped with hot coals. The seventh apple never showed up. It was a gift *taken*.

Barbara recalls too how they finally bought a new house and prepared to move. Barbara says the pictures, one by one, began to fall off the walls. The glass never broke; but they no longer could keep pictures on the wall. It never happened until they decided to leave. Barbara remarks, "We felt the house loved us, and didn't want us to leave."

8

Angels

The *Reader's Digest* of October 2000 reported that an astounding 84% of Americans believe that miracles happen, and 48% believe they have themselves experienced or witnessed one—that is nearly every other person in this country. A possible explanation is that souls on the other side of death's veil look out for the living.

The current flood of angel stories in magazines across America also suggests what might be called "selective noticing." When in distress, we may gratefully and unsuspiciously accept the help of strangers, then return to our concerns. When we look up, they have gone without our having noticed their departure—and it seems they have just disappeared. Probably in many cases there is a logical, earthly explanation. Judge for yourself. All these are stories told to me by friends who have never otherwise lied to me, so I can't think they are doing so now.

I have a friend, Clyde Beck, who lives in McDowell, Virginia. Clyde is first a fine artist, well-known in northern Virginia, but also works as a building constructor. His life has been chockful of psychic experiences, and he appears in many of these stories. He and I share an intense interest in unexplainable things.

One day he brought a friend from Constance, Germany, named Berthold Maier, to my house for lunch. Maier tells me how he stopped at a railroad barrier one day to wait for a train to go by, his small son in the car with him. Berthold recounts that he got out of the car and went back to talk to a friend in a car behind theirs. Apparently his son, not yet two, escaped from the car while the two men talked, and was going under the barrier towards the train, unnoticed. When Berthold looked up, his son was toddling towards the onrushing train, too far away for Berthold to get to him. Suddenly, a woman ran up out of nowhere and snatched the child back from the track. Berthold reached them, overwhelmed by gratitude, guilt and fear, and gathered the child in his arms, weeping. He looked around to thank the woman, but no one was there—and Berthold vows there was nowhere she could have gone. She simply disappeared.

On August 25, 1955, my friend Basil "Skip" Davis of Lexington was recuperating from an operation in Memorial Hospital in Roanoke, Virginia. In the long night, when he was ill, a nurse with long black hair and in a blue uniform with no name tag showed up to hold his hand. Her presence made him feel better. Next morning when he asked around so he could thank her, it turned out that no one fitting that description had been on duty that night—or ever.

But he learned from other nurses that he was the fourth patient to have reported ministration from this nameless angelic nurse. That started him going to church and reading the Bible, but he remained unsaved. That was the event, though, that got him to thinking about God.

Another synchronicity: one day as I visited with a new Hospice patient, in strolled Skip, who turned out to be my patient's son-in-law!

A woman I met at a book-signing for my book *The Man Who Wanted Seven Wives*, in Lewisburg, West Virginia, told me that she has had two angelic interventions in her life. Linda Hammer is her name. The first story began when she got a call one Sunday that her mother and father had been in a serious car wreck and her father killed. Her mother, though alive, was so severely injured that she had been helicoptered to the nearest trauma center, at the Johns Hopkins Hospital in Baltimore.

Linda had never been to Baltimore, but knew she had to get to her mother. She and her husband set out in their car from West Virginia immediately, using only a general road map of the eastern United States, with few details, and none about Baltimore. She figured they'd get directions later. They took I-64 east to I-81, then I-70 across Maryland, stopping west of Baltimore at a visitors' center, which, frustratingly, turned out to be closed for the weekend.

Driving on, at the edge of Baltimore, they stopped at a service station, bought gas, and asked for directions. But not only was the attendant behind bullet-proof glass, he apparently spoke no English—and either could not or would not help.

Now frustrated, Linda noticed a white van that had pulled in behind them. A blond man with long hair got out and said a puzzling thing to her: "You want maps? I have maps."

She briefly looked for a name on the van, or some identification, but could find none—while the amiable young man rummaged under the driver's seat and came up with a map of the city of Baltimore. He pointed out the route to the trauma center, and headed for the restroom.

Linda and her husband studied the route and marked it on the map, and when they looked up to thank the kind man, he and the van were both gone. They never saw him come back from the restroom, or heard him start his van up or pull out. They agreed that the encounter felt strange. They made it to the hospital without incident.

After a difficult recuperation, Linda's mother recovered. Only later did Linda decide the man must have been an angel.

Linda believes she had a second angelic intervention that saved her life. She recalls the day she was home alone in her country house washing curtains as a thunder storm approached. She was standing on top of the dryer, taking down the laundry room curtains, when she heard a voice call her name loudly.

She dropped the curtains, hopped off the dryer, and had just reached the laundry room door when there was a huge blast, and a bright light. Lightning had struck the dryer on which she had been standing only a second before—and wrecked it entirely, even melting the nylon curtains she'd dropped on top. She could never identify the voice she heard so clearly as even male or female—and a thorough search found no one else anywhere around the house or property.

Richard Moore told me of seeing an angel in his room once when he was a child and ill. He went and got his mother, who came when he told her an angel was in his room, but when they got back, to his mother's annoyance, the angel had vanished.

In 1967 I had six-plus pounds of breast tissue removed, in an operation called a reduction mammaplasty. In those days it was a major operation requiring three weeks' hospitalization. I was in the old Jefferson Hospital in Roanoke, which was in its last days. Cockroaches shared the night with me. The nursing staff was minimal. Rules were lax. On the night after my surgery, I was dreadfully ill from anesthesia, and was strapped down to the bed, swaddled in bandages, my chest full of 500 stitches that might tear out if I moved. All I could do was to groan, "I'm going to throw up." Every single time I did, a woman arrived to hold the bedpan for me.

I never vomited on myself, and no nurse checked on me in the night. The lady explained that she was sitting with her mother who was dying in the room next to me.

Next day when I was feeling better we chatted and soon became friends. I was so grateful for her ministrations. I never until lately thought of Lewise Parsley as an angel, but we were friends until her death, having lunch together in the following years when I'd go to Roanoke for something. But in that long night she appeared out of nowhere to take care of me.

My definition of angels changed when I recalled this story.

Aunt Polly has a daughter, my cousin Posey Curry Neidigh. Posey's best friend took a rafting trip on her honeymoon in Idaho. Their raft tipped over in some rapids into icy water, the bride being tossed out of the raft and thrown against a rock by the current. The others, including her husband, were washed far downstream into stiller pools. As the young wife clung to the rock, unable to get herself unwedged, a tall young man struggled through the swift water and boulders, and dragged her to safety on the nearby shore.

Heading downstream to rejoin her friends, she looked up to thank her rescuer, but he had vanished. None of the others ever saw him, and assumed that she had gotten out of the treacherous current by herself. She, however, knowing what she knows, is convinced she was saved by an angel.

9

In and Out of the Body

Three times people (all women) have told me, "I can fly." Barbara Goldsten is one of them. "I think it's called an Out of Body Experience. It happens at night when I'm asleep. I've never left the house. I used to fly through and around the chandelier. I learned what it was called from an article, but I'd done it all my life before that. Once when we'd had a birthday party, I flew all around the balloons that were still stuck to the ceiling. I know which high shelves have to be dusted; I see them from the top.

"It's like swimming in air, you can feel the air go by. You can make your 'body' move the way you want it to go, by dropping an arm or leg. I can look down at myself and Joe in bed. It never occurs to me to go outside of the room, except maybe into an adjoining room."

Another woman in an Elderhostel class of mine, Harrison Bedloe, told me that as a child she flew at night around her Maryland neighborhood. She flew into people's dining rooms, and even their bedrooms, so that she always knew when families had fights, or when a couple were divorcing. She knew people's secrets and what the inside of every neighborhood house looked like. However, when she reached adolescence, she quit doing it, and has never been able to remember since how she did it. I'm reminded of James Barrie's *Peter Pan* as I hear her story.

Burwell Wingfield tells me that at times of stress he has separated from his body. The conditions have been that he is tired, stressed, trying to finish a paper or study for a difficult exam. He has been able to look down on his own body sitting at a desk, while hovering perhaps a foot above his perfectly clear body below.

My friend Clyde Beck decided he wanted to go out of body. His first attempt was successful: leaving his body, he perceived a "guide,"—a blonde child who explained things to him as they went. She took him to a house where he'd lived as a child, and said they could enter through the wall. Clyde doubted that, and held back; so the little girl explained that, *at this particular part of the wall, there had once been a window,* so it was easier to get through than solid wall. The next thing he knew, Clyde was in his old living room.

The house appeared abandoned and dirty. Determined to gather proof of his visit, he found what he thought was a piece of chalk on the mantle, and made a white line on the wall next to the mantelpiece. He remembers nothing of the experience after that.

Anxious for verification, Clyde soon found the time to go back and see the house. Indeed it was empty and rundown, just as he'd seen. He is a builder, and was able to examine the place the child told him there had once been a window, and that also proved correct. But when he went to look at the mark he'd made with the chalk, he found not a white line, but a black one. This experience convinced him of the reality of the "visit." But he still wonders about the incorrect color of his chalk mark. I still wonder at my vision of gin instead of vodka bottles; my grandfather Marston "saw" his watch in snow, but found it in grass.

My younger brother Peter Letcher had a most unusual out-of-body experience. He and his then-wife Nancy went to gather some apples on some land off the Blue Ridge Parkway occupied by an unpleasant neighbor whose son was in prison for shooting and killing two people. That entire family tended to violence as the choice method for solving difficulties. Thus Pete took a gun along for protection, even though the ownership of the old orchard was in dispute.

On this day, Pete and Nancy were gathering apples when the erratic neighbor appeared in a pickup truck, jumped out, pumped up a carbine, and pointed the gun first at Pete, saying, "I've got you now, you S.O.B!" Turning to Nancy, he yelled, "And you too, Bitch!"

Pete grabbed his pistol and cocked it. At that instant, he found himself suddenly sitting about thirty feet up in an apple tree, coolly observing the situation below, without an adrenalin rush or any anxiety—which he would have expected to feel, as he had many times during his service in Vietnam.

He watched the neighbor shoot out the window of his (Pete's) truck; then watched *himself* shoot the neighbor in the face; and finally saw *himself* step forward to shoot him again to finish him off. All this he saw clearly, while also seeing his wife Nancy crouched terrified behind their truck.

Suddenly back in his body, my brother realized that none of this had actually happened. Instead, the irate neighbor lowered his gun, and backed off, though still yelling obscenities at them. No shots were fired; the neighbor stumbled into his pickup and tore off, jerking his truck into reverse. To this day, Pete wonders what the neighbor "saw" that changed his mind—and wonders if he himself watched *an alternate future* in those few seconds.

My brother John (Johnny) Letcher sailed solo, using only celestial navigation, from California to Hawaii in 1963 when he was twenty-one, on a twenty-foot sailboat called the "Island Girl." The trip was impressive enough that *Life* Magazine did a story on it. The next summer, he sailed the same boat back from Hawaii to Sitka, Alaska, and eventually back to California. Twice, he was in grave mortal danger, and both times he feels he left his body.

While sailing north from Hawaii to Alaska, he endured a week of stormy weather, and when the skies cleared the wind went into the west and blew a gale for eighteen hours. He had to stay at the helm the entire time, with no sail, steering the boat downwind. The seas were large, with many breaking crests.

Fifteen hours into the experience, he saw a wave approaching much higher and steeper than the others, nearly a mile away. It crested and fell in a huge plunging breaker that would have likely destroyed both boat and sailor had it hit him. As he rose to each wave's crest, Johnny could see back to where it had broken, a great patch of pale aquamarine foam in the otherwise deep blue water. He clearly recalls this scene from about thirty feet above and slightly behind his own head. He was watching himself.

The big wave did not reach him, and three hours later the sea subsided enough to allow him to grab some food and rest. The next day when he fixed his position, it appeared he had been traveling over a group of seamounts—underwater mountains that raise the depth of the ocean to only about five hundred feet, interrupt swells and promote waves breaking.

The following summer Johnny had another, similar experience—and to this day he remembers both events from the perspective of being about thirty feet up in the air, looking down dispassionately and calmly at his body struggling to keep the boat aright.

The second experience happened just at dawn. There was a lot of wind, and he had spent the night dragging a sea anchor to stabilize his boat. The first big wave came and broke into his cockpit, depositing so much water it broke his cockpit slides, the closures between the cockpit and lower deck. He then had to scrabble and struggle to haul the sea anchor in so the boat could ride the waves instead of being swamped by the next wave, which might have filled the cockpit and sunk the boat entirely. Again, during the most dangerous phase, he watched himself impassively from above as he worked at fever pitch below to save his boat.

Interestingly, a week later when he reached Santa Barbara and called his fiancee, she asked, "Did something happen to you at dawn about a week ago?" Pati, a thousand miles away, explained that she had been jolted awake with a terrifying feeling that Johnny was in grave danger. She knew something was wrong—and fifteen minutes later she felt it was over, and that he was safe, and went back to sleep.

A locally famous case of psychic detection occurred in Staunton, Virginia, in 1974, and was reported in the papers. A young girl, Debbie Back, had disappeared from her home some years before. She had never returned, and there were no credible theories about what had happened to her. That year Blue Ridge Community College sponsored a parapsychology symposium, (led by my friend David McKnight) and among the invited speakers was a noted psychic from New England. A local police official asked the psychic to try to locate the little girl, but nothing came of that.

Reading a newspaper account of the policeman's attempt to solve the Back case using a psychic, a certain Staunton woman called David McKnight, head of the symposium, saying that she had had a vision of Debbie being in liquid with lime over her. David didn't know what to do with the information, and told only his wife Mary.

Renewed publicity in the mysterious case drew a police detective from elsewhere in Virginia to the area who dug under an abandoned outhouse in the back yard of the family's home as an obvious place to look—and indeed found the child's skeleton in the lime-covered liquid below. Though the woman who called David didn't "see" an outhouse, what she did see was accurate. The police detective had acted on common sense, having no psychic clues.

So how had the psychic woman "seen" the body? Had she gone out of her body looking? Or could the police officer's "common sense" have been psyche at work? Marilyn Greene, in *Finder*, argues that the two often are one and the same.

Joyce Moore was living in married students' quarters with her husband near their university. He went to play bridge one weekend, and partnered with a fellow he had not met before. A few days later, Joyce's husband invited the new partner and his wife to visit them. During the visit, the man and his wife sat without saying a word, which made Joyce feel nervous. The nervous feeling escalated into weirdness. Suddenly Joyce found herself hovering in the corner of the living room, looking down at four people, herself one of them, from the ceiling. After a while she was suddenly back in her body again.

She *had* to talk about it. So she did, and the silent couple listened. Then the husband of the couple got up and just walked out, leaving Joyce to feel even more uncomfortable there with her husband and the strange woman.

But soon the man returned, and still silent, handed her a book: *You Forever*, by Tuesday Lobsang Rampa. She read it eagerly, and learned from the book how to leave her body at will. After several years she quit doing it because to her it "always felt a little creepy." Now twenty years have passed and Joyce says she can no longer remember how to get out of body.

As a child, my mushroom-hunting companion Burwell Wingfield was once ill in a hospital. He woke up thirsty, and could not seem to attract a nurse's attention. So he got out of bed, left the room, and spied a nurses' station. As he passed the station, the nurse on duty appeared not to notice him. About then, he looked around and spied a water bubbler down a hall perpendicular to the one he stood in, so he went and got a drink, and returned to his bed.

When his mother visited him later, and was thirsty, he told her where the fountain was. A nurse, overhearing, asked, "How did you know that?" He replied, "I've been there, I got up and got some water last night."

"No way!" the nurse said. "You couldn't have gotten out of those restraints. You haven't been out of bed since you got here."

These folks are not liars. Though it's never happened to me, I believe that OOBE's are just another piece of evidence that part of us can, and does, separate from our bodies sometimes. Perhaps it happens to us all at death.

10

Near-Death Events

Because medical science can now bring dying people back from the brink of death, there are increasing numbers of stories, and books, of glimpses of the other side of death before returning to earth-life. Scientists know that glutagen starvation of the brain leads to visions. If we study the history of visionaries, perhaps their brains, deprived of glutagen by many methods—starvation, fasting, beatings, torture, extreme stress, or drugs—led them to their visions. All-night vigils, chanting, singing, and drumming, all apparently lead to an increase of carbon dioxide in the brain, as do breathing exercises—which also are implicated in rebirthing therapy as well as many other anomalous events. It is apparently not difficult to change our body chemistry to enhance visions.

Sherwin Nuland, in his book *How We Die*, writes, "People who bleed to death hyperventilate, trying to make up for the plummeting volume of blood by short, fast breaths, as if that will bring it more oxygen. Heart rate surges. The heart and then brain slow. A flood of natural opiates called endorphins washes over the brain, bringing on tranquility and hallucinations." In Nuland's view, these are the "near-death experiences," the visions of light and sense of floating reported by people wrested back from death. Read the following stories and see if you agree.

Do spirits really come to collect the dying and aid their transitions? For several years, I have been a volunteer and board member of the Rockbridge Area Hospice. It is commonplace to have a dying patient, usually within forty-eight hours of death, announce a visit by a relative or friend who has died, by saying, "Oh, here is Mother!" or "My husband was here last night."

What do we involved with Hospice make of this? It's such a consistent event reported by nurses and volunteers that to say it's just the patient's brain misfiring, or a lack of oxygen causing hallucinations in the dying brain seems too easy. Why doesn't the dying brain "see" some live person? Or pink elephants? *Why are the visitors always people who have already passed on?*

At Hospice we work hard to make sure our patients are at peace, their affairs settled, their physical discomfort allayed, and any emotional pain dealt with. *Appearances from friends or relatives who have died occur so consistently that it is on the list of signs of imminent death that Hospice workers and volunteers learn.*

One day I had an amazing conversation with a Hospice patient I'd been visiting as a volunteer for nearly six months. She had congestive heart failure, but seemed to be doing fine. She didn't appear to be dying at all. That day, Anne happened to ask me, "What are you writing now?" Mostly she forgot I am a writer, and we talked about all sorts of things, but her memory came and went. We had tea parties, pleasant chats about the past, and I read a lot to her. She talked about her early days as a social worker in Texas during the Depression. But we'd never talked about the Afterlife.

So I said I was writing a book about the paranormal, things like near-death experiences and ghost stories. When her eyes lit up, I figured it was okay to go on. I asked her if she had any personal paranormal experiences she could tell me about.

"My sister came to see me just after her death," she replied. "I wasn't asleep, and she was there, looking as real as in real life. She was as real as you are."

"What do you think happens after death?" I asked.

She thought a few moments. "Whatever you think will happen," she said.

"What do *you* think will happen?" I persisted.

"I think all my people will be there, the ones that have gone on before, to help me over," she said.

"Who's the first person you're going to see?" I asked, because her face was animated with pleasure.

She lifted her shoulders in a characteristic girlish gesture of anticipation. "Pat!" she said. Her husband.

When I got word of Anne's sudden decline and death two days later, I could not be anything but happy for her.

This same woman's second son was coming to see her the weekend she unexpectedly died. Anne had been doing fine except for her troubling shortness of breath. Her first son was already there from California. On the day she died, she went downhill rapidly, going from being ambulatory to dying in three hours. When it was clear that Anne was dying, her eldest son called his brother's cell phone to report their mother's precipitous decline. Her second son, already on the road, told me three days later that when he got this alarming news, in his mind he began a conversation with his mother—and clearly felt and heard her response. At a certain moment while he was still driving, he said he felt her death, and sensed her spirit leave her body with a delighted whoosh! He noted the time. When he arrived in Lexington, he learned that his impression was correct. His mother had died at the moment he felt her leave.

I have a story of my own about Anne's death. I was at a writers' gathering when she died, but Hospice got hold of me there to tell me, as she had been my patient, and death caught up with her so unexpectedly. I was shocked, because she'd been so well during my visit two days before. At the time I got the call that she had died, I had to concentrate on other things, and did not go to bed that night until 1:00 a.m. The room was hot, and so I opened a window. The curtains hung limp; it was a still night. As I got into bed, my thoughts returned to Anne. I was lying on my side facing the open window, glad for fresh air. I asked silently, "Anne, are you okay?"

At that moment, the curtains ballooned inward, and I had a sense of sparkling, bright, pink energy swooping in, full of joy and freedom. Then the curtains fell limp again. I lay awake as long as I could, watching to see if there was in fact some breeze or wind causing the curtains to move. While I watched, there was no more movement—though it may have been only a minute or two until I fell asleep.

One day as I walked in the front door to sit with George W, dying of cancer, he said to me, "Keith was right there where you're standing, just a while ago." I asked who Keith was, as I knew the rest of George's family. He explained that it was his mentor, the man who'd hired him to teach, his department chairman. I'd known *that* Keith, and said, "Oh, of course!" when I remembered that he had died some years before.

George went on: "At Keith's funeral, I saw him dancing on his coffin." Now George was medicated with morphine, so it is arguable that he could have been talking nonsense. But it happens consistently to our patients, usually within about forty-eight hours of death. George died about two days later.

Menno Kinsinger of Stuart's Draft, Virginia, was named for the founder of the Mennonites, a Dutchman named Menno Simons. Kinsinger is an architectural restorer, responsible for moving the first of three European homesteads to the famous Frontier Culture Museum at Staunton, Virginia, and reassembling them. He was working as a stone mason on another European building at Explore Park in Roanoke at the time of his being struck down and nearly killed by spinal meningitis. He's retired now, since his brush with death.

Of his life and career as a Christian artisan, he says, "I wanted His touch on everything I did. I always felt blessed to have my talents as a restorer and stonemason." Kinsinger is a member of the Beachy Amish (founded by a man named Beachy), a sub-sect of the Amish, one step more modern than the old order Amish, who still use no electricity, drive only horses and buggies, and have no telephones.

Menno feels he has been saved by God twelve times in his life. Though he believes he was spared to *tell the world* what he discovered in his visions, he is glad that I will write his story. To him, referring to "I" feels immodest, and so he doesn't want to write it himself.

Menno is a bearded man, young-looking for his age, solidly built, rosy-cheeked and bright-eyed.

I apologize for arriving early for the interview, but he says, "I always like to get places early," letting me know that Godly industry demands promptness, perhaps even favors the early bird.

In our first few minutes together, he comments on youth today, "People call their children kids, then wonder why they act like goats." He tells me how one of his own children used to ask, "Oh Daddy, do I have to do it?" of some activity the child preferred not to do. And he would reply, "As soon as you want to, you don't *have* to."

Retired now, Menno is busier than ever, participating in a prison ministry. Of his prisoner friends, he says, "The reason they are in prison is that no one took the initiative to teach them when they were young."

I take down the story Menno tells often, wants to tell, needs to tell. "How," he asks rhetorically, "can I begin to exemplify how great is God's glory?"

"I was working at Explore Park in Roanoke, doing stonework for the Blue Tavern. I experienced symptoms I thought were a heart attack. It was about three o'clock. I prayed, and down I went. But I pulled out that time."

A week later he got ill at work, and barely managed to negotiate the eighty-nine miles of highway between his job and home. "I was working in a field, and Mama (his wife) had driven the truck the ninety miles home. I drove and pushed myself, crying, to get home. Mama treated my ear all night, but the next morning my head felt full of needles. The earache was gone, but what a headache! I fell against the wall. I pled to God to go Home, and that's the last I recall for six and a half days.

"Later I learned that the rescue squad came and took me to the hospital, where I was diagnosed with spinal meningitis. The local hospital thought I should be taken to Charlottesville, but they couldn't get Pegasus (the rescue helicopter) over the mountain because it was snowing. At 1 a.m., the doctors told my family, 'He won't live.' For four days following, my temperature was at 104, even with ice packs along my sides. They planned to put me on a bed of ice. My body, when I was aware of it, was twisted like a rope, just pure pain.

"Sometime in there I awoke to see a bright half-moon of light at the end of a dark tunnel. 'I'm still alive,' I realized, though I had prayed for death. But a voice said, 'I still have work for you.' I felt a pulling, a tugging, at my heart. 'Do my will,' the voice said. He understood my frail little body.

"Sometime later, to my right it got so bright I could hardly look. But I did look, and there right in front of me was a gorgeous city, so beautiful, with straight golden streets, and beautiful buildings. There were no chimneys, or storm windows, or gutters.

"I was so startled! I glanced down. I was standing by a riverside looking, with this river in between it and me. The river was deep, maybe 150 feet wide, beautiful, full, sturdy clear clean water, and I wanted to get to that city. I planned to just dive in and swim across. My right foot was actually out over the bank. I was stunned. *This is Home*, I knew.

"But suddenly, a pair of hands at my waist dragged me back just as I was going in. And that voice said, 'Remember, I still have work for you to do.' It was the saddest moment of my life, not to be able to go there.

"Finally I came to in grimacing pain; I couldn't breathe, and pled for mercy. To my left, about 75 or 100 feet away, I saw a beautiful halo. Down at the bottom I saw our dear Savior Jesus on his knees, moaning and groaning to break your heart. It was just like the Garden of Eden: there was a palm tree there, and an olive tree.

"He was pleading of His Father to let the cup pass from Him. I saw Him sweat as I have never seen another man sweat. Sweat was actually pouring off His body. Not blood, but sweat. And He said, 'Father, not my will but Thine be done.' I felt like that was a knife in my heart. I've said that many times, but I didn't really mean it.

"Jesus knew He would soon hear them say, 'We want Him out of the way,' but they had no idea. They said, not knowing what they said, 'Let His blood be on us and on our children.'

"The Bible says He took the sting out of death for us. That sting was, Jesus had been in Heaven, He knew Heaven, and He knew His Father was going to have to step back long enough for Him to die.

"I saw how I'd been so vague in my understanding. I saw how at death, there is not a separation but a reunion. When He made that statement, angels stepped in, brightly dressed, with crowns on their heads, and wings. They put their hands on His head. It was so awesome.

"When I give this account, I always ask if there are any questions. One time I did, and afterwards, a little boy in the audience asked, "Were you in your body or out?" All I could say was 'I never had a dream even close to this.'

"Later I was in terrible pain again. I was rolled up and twisted like a cloth when the Lord says, `My friend, remember that all those who go to Hell will have this to contend with forever, no respite. But for you this is foreshortening.'

"After I came to, I saw a picture of John standing looking into the third Hell, and he saw there 144,000. He showed me a multitude of people, another group as couldn't be numbered. The Elder says, 'Who are those?' John says, 'You know who they are. Those are the innumerable ones who are washed in the blood of the lamb, who are also saved. If 144,000 can go by the straight gate and the narrow way, how many more can go the other way?'"

A neighbor interrupts our interview, bringing a bag of eleven fat tadpoles for Menno's pond. The neighbor has a cleft palate, and has obviously not had speech therapy or corrective surgery. He is difficult to understand, but chats a few minutes. The two men josh: Menno commented on the bag of polliwogs, "They don't have any raincoats."

His friend glances outside. "Soon they'll need some. Heard one bullfrog out there last evening."

"Well," Menno said, "my five-year old granddaughter caught a big old catfish last night."

They joke about Menno's upcoming chiropractic session to correct a recent injury. "They need a parts department for old people," the neighbor remarks.

"New parts or used?" Menno says right back. They laugh, and the neighbor leaves to release the tadpoles into the pond. Menno explains how he'd had hundreds of frogs last year, but a neighbor boy asked to gig some of them, and cleaned him out. Took every one. Then he leaned back and continued his story.

"One day I felt something so familiar I tried to open my eyes. I did, and it was my wife's dear hand. I went back to sleep.

"Finally one day I woke up and asked how long I'd been sick. Six-and-a-half-days.

"On the day I married my wife, in 1957, I had prayed for a

good wife, and when the preacher got to the place in the ceremony where it asked if I would care for her in sickness and health, I felt a sudden shock like lightning enter my body at the right shoulder, go through it at an angle, and go out my left knee. My whole body shook. It made the hair stand up on my body. I read that to mean that something was going to happen to my wife. I thought it meant she would die young. Nearly forty years later, I was the one who nearly died, February 7, 1997."

And he tells me a final vision he had: "One day since then I was talking to this individual, and I had my hand out like this, and had just asked, 'Why does God even notice this lump of clay?'—when I saw clearly something float down between us like a strip of cheesecloth. In the middle in black writing, I read, 'I didn't do this for you; I did this to strengthen the faith of those that pray.'"

Aunt Polly told me that when Mama bore a pair of twins in China (they were conjoined twins and premature), hemorrhaged and nearly died, and was ill for months afterwards, she had a near-death experience: she told Polly that in the crisis of her illness she had been in some glorious peaceful place that was like a garden from which she most emphatically did not want to return, but was told she must. My mother never told me this story, and it's only fair to report that I heard it from Polly only recently.

But may I add that my mother seemed so brave to me, saying continually that she had no fear of death. She was uncomfortable enough that death seemed welcome. When people would come to visit, saying "I'll pray for you, Betty," she'd say to me after they left, "Only you and I know what to pray for."

Nearly ten years ago, Peter Ross of Lexington was in an automobile accident. His wife was driving, and his baby daughter was in the back seat. When the car came to a sudden stop from 55

miles an hour, Pete's seat belt did not work, and he was jarred badly.

Pete got out of the car and got his little girl, but as soon as he did, he realized that something was wrong with him. Nonetheless, he called a wrecker, got the car out of the ditch, and drove his wife and daughter on to Lynchburg, their destination. After doing whatever they had gone there for, he drove them back, a trip of around 100 miles, though he had an increasing sense that something was awfully wrong.

A week later, he got ready to go to work, brushed his teeth, and walked down into the kitchen. Suddenly one arm and one leg gave way, and he could not speak.

His wife called 911, and he was taken to the Lexington hospital, where a doctor gave him "wrong medicine." He kept getting worse; and when he was nearly dead, he was helicoptered to Charlottesville, a half-hour air trip. When the helicopter arrived, Ross was pronounced dead.

At the hospital, his body was turned over to the coroner on duty. What Pete remembers is that he "went up two stories to a place that was somewhere I didn't want to be." As far as he knows today, he was in his body. He felt as if he was.

An alert doctor found him in the coroner's area several hours later, his temperature having dropped perilously low—but the doctor recognized that he wasn't dead. That is all Pete knew until he awoke, paralysed, without speech.

He was in the hospital six months, trying to relearn everything. Full recovery took five years.

Pete tells me that in the time he was "dead," he was shown thirty-two lifetimes in different bodies, seven as females, and that he saw and visited with his father and brother, who are both deceased.

He feels blessed to be alive, and feels strongly the lessons learned from his "death" and nearly impossible climb back to functional life. *"Don't hurt anybody,"* is the big one.

Now Pete Ross feels that he is mentally sixty or seventy years old, wiser than a man half that age, from five years of just listening to people, without his own voice to respond.

Pete has become an avid believer in the Afterlife. "*When you know, you know,*" he says. "*Heaven is another dimension, that's all. Time is nothing.*"

Two months before I interviewed him he finally got his voice back. He says, "When I didn't have a voice, I didn't want to listen. But now that I have a voice, I don't want to talk. I just want to *be*."

Mary McKnight had a near-death experience just after brain surgery in a Canadian hospital for excision of a brain tumor that nearly killed her. Furthermore, there are verifiable elements to her near-death experience.

As she remembers it, she went out of her body and floated up to the ceiling of the Intensive Care Unit of the hospital where she was. In a bed near to hers she noticed someone surrounded by medical staff, and she sensed it was a man having a heart attack, obviously fighting for his life, and she wished that she could help him. At the moment of her wish, she saw a rainbow arc down from the ceiling to him, and watched as he sat up.

During the same experience, she saw her grandfather, who had died at seventy. He approached and hugged her, then danced with her, and said, laughing as at a joke, "I am ninety-three years old now!" He looked much younger. Seeing a radiant light, she moved toward it, and heard a voice say, "God is not so much a Trinity as a Magnanimity. God is in everything."

She recounted the experience to her father when he visited her in the hospital, and her father confirmed that indeed her grandfather would be ninety-three now if he were alive.

A second confirmation occurred after Mary was up and around, six weeks later. She went with her father to get new glasses from an optometrist her father knew. The optometrist mentioned a mutual friend of theirs who had recently made a miraculous and total recovery from a heart attack. Had, in fact, just sat up, and was, against all logic, found to be recovered.

Oh, yes," Mary's father said, "I know about that. He was in a bed near Mary in Intensive Care."

Some years ago, when I was reading through scores of diaries by nineteenth century Virginia women, which I hoped to write a book about, I came upon a curious story. The young diarist, during the Civil War, wrote that a woman in the neighborhood had died, but that in her final moments, the woman and said, "Oh, there are Johnny and Joe! I want to go with them!"

The diarist went on to report that Johnny and Joe were her twin sons, and that Johnny had been killed in the Battle of New Market—but that Joe was thought to be alive.

A little later, the diarist reported, the woman died. Next day, to everyone's surprise, word came that her son Joe had been killed a few days before her passing.

LuAnne Patrick was sitting with her then mother-in-law in Waynesboro, Virginia, the day before Mrs. Milford died. Her mother-in-law started talking incoherently about Lee and Sunny and Pat as if they were in the room with her. When her husband came back, LuAnne asked him who Lee and Sunny and Pat were, for she'd certainly never heard of them. Her husband said, "Oh, where'd you hear about them? They're three friends of Mom's that were all killed in an automobile accident years ago."

11

Poetic Justice, 1959

In 1959 I graduated from Hollins College still a rationalist, and went to Johns Hopkins for an MA in Philosophy from the Writing Seminars. I loved living in Baltimore; I met lots of folks, got a job singing in the famous Peabody's Bookshop, and in the three years I lived there, I completed my degree the first, and taught at two private schools for a year each. For a time I roomed with an elderly wealthy woman who had distant connections with my mother's family, and lived all alone in a real stone castle-like mansion. "Aunt Eleanor" had had a tragic life, outliving both her husband and their two children. She spoke openly of communing with the spirits of both her dead children, and had a semi-provable story: a remarkable experience in the 1930's in which time apparently got jumbled.

She was in Johns Hopkins University Hospital recuperating from surgery when she awakened in her hospital room to see three men standing near her bed discussing something with a good deal of urgency. As she listened, she noticed they were dressed at least several decades out of fashion, in what she decided looked like golfing outfits from around 1910. The only thing she could recall later of their conversation was a name, which I think was Tully Cummings.

Not understanding what the men were doing in her room, Aunt Eleanor attempted to say something. At that, all three started, turned, looked at her, clearly surprised, and then vanished. Just disappeared. Later, she tried to gain access to hospital records to find out if a man named Tully Cummings ever occupied that room, and her information was inconclusive. A man by the name of Tully Cummings had once been a patient at Hopkins, but she could learn nothing beyond that. When she told me the story in 1959, she looked off in the distance and remarked, "What I've always wondered is, what did those men see?"

How I wish I had taken Aunt Eleanor more seriously! She had lost her daughter to polio, and her son in an auto accident in which my mother's brother, my uncle Jack, had been the driver. Afterwards, she sort of adopted Jack as her own, and that is how the families got connected. She felt she'd had clear and unmistakable contacts with both her children after their deaths, visions with messages in both cases. These visions had allowed her to continue more serenely, to better tolerate not only the early loss of her husband, but also the untimely loss of both her children. It was typical of her that she later "adopted" Jack and treated him as her own.

The time has come to tell you my perhaps-ghost story from my Baltimore days, though the experience did not seem supernatural to me at the time—*because*, I now think, I wasn't a believer.

The story starts a long time before I got to Baltimore. On a rainy October night in 1849, a man wasted in body and mind was discovered on a Baltimore street, possibly the victim of foul play, certainly the victim of physical and psychological disintegration. He was taken to a hospital where he died four days later of "congestion of the brain." The man was Edgar Allan Poe, and his body was quietly buried a few days later in the Greene Street Cemetery, not half a mile from the place where he had been found. The seasons changed, and changed again; the city grew, and life went on.

Exactly 110 years later, on a bright day in October of 1959, a melodramatic and reverent graduate student, on her own in a great city for the first time, left the corridors of Gilman Hall at Johns Hopkins for the afternoon to make what she deemed an appropriate pilgrimage to Edgar Allan Poe's grave.

After all, once the young woman I was then had made the discovery in high school that Poe was the teacher's favorite author, I had easily gotten A's in English. All I needed to do was imitate Poe's language and his gloomy views of the world in order to elicit swoons of delight from Miss Mary Hamilton, dictator queen of Lexington High School. She's the one who let me do my senior thesis on witchcraft, too.

I majored in English and Latin in college, then sought a further degree so that I could teach, which is what brought me to Hopkins in the autumn of my twenty-first year. So it seemed appropriate that I go to pay homage to the man who had insured that I would later become an English major, and someday an English teacher.

The small Greene Street Cemetery was in terrible shape. Grave-holes lay sunken and empty, tombstones were broken or overturned, and the grass wanted trimming. A sign pointed the way to Poe's grave. I followed a ruined path that wound around to the far corner of the small burial ground, and found the modest monument that marked his resting place. I stood in the afternoon sun, looking up at the buildings stretching skyward on three sides, and back at the brick wall beyond which was the city street. Already the part of the cemetery where I stood was sliding into shade. Outside, cars purred by, buses backfired and changed gears, the city's familiar tintinnabulation.

I had that feeling that must be common to those who visit the tombs of famous people: the embarrassment that one may appear superstitious by being there in the first place; the effort to think whatever lofty thoughts inspired the visit; the helpless sense that one's presence is totally superfluous for surely, wherever Poe was, he was not there! And here I was, representative of that rational daytime world Poe hated, come to gape. So it was like an echo of my own thoughts when I heard a voice say, "He isn't there." I had thought until that moment that I was alone.

I whirled, in an instant assessed the interloper: smaller than I was, if it came to that; old, possibly forty; and curious looking, gnomish. His hair was long for the time, and the top of his head was bald. His color was bad, as if he spent all his hours indoors. He went on, gesturing vaguely across the way, "He's buried over there." The grave he indicated several feet away was marked with another's name. I am sure I frowned, a bit irritated to have my meditations, however mundane, interrupted. But I was nonetheless curious. Had I come face to face with a modern Roderick Usher?

Charles S, he said. (Charles Stewart was his name). He was the caretaker of the cemetery. Relief loosened my tongue, and I had to ask how such an error had occurred.

Perhaps I was the first tourist he'd gotten for some time. Around 1900, he related, the city of Baltimore had passed an ordinance that all cemeteries within the city limits that did not have churches on the grounds would be destroyed to provide space for new office buildings and stores, as the old part of the city grew more crowded.

Yet the patrons of Greene Street Cemetery did not want their relatives' remains disturbed. What could they do to prevent the old cemetery's being razed in the name of progress? They answered the challenge by erecting a church hastily, directly on top of part of the cemetery, moving some of the graves quickly, as it was necessary to dig a foundation for the church. They had to work so rapidly that there was little regard for accuracy. Poe had never, Mr. Stewart, gotten moved back.

Mr. Stewart said that he had a grandfather buried here, and when he had become caretaker, he had contrived to retrieve his grandfather's Civil War sword from that Colonel Stewart's crypt. Would I care to see it? It had been buried with his grandfather for more than half a century. By then I was hooked. The Civil War sword looked like every other one I'd seen; and of course I had no proof that this curious chatty man had really robbed his ancestor's grave.

Mr. Stewart was, he continued, in addition to curating the cemetery, the curator of the ship *USS Constellation* which stood in the Baltimore harbor; he said they could not keep night watchmen because the ghost of a young sailor that haunted the ship scared them all away. He told me of how, recently, a matron touring the ship insisted that she had been shown around by "a young sailor in an old fashioned looking sailor outfit, with a strange accent." None of the guides even remotely fit the description the lady gave, and none of the guides wore costumes.

The most vivid of the episodes I remember: a new nightwatchman in the long succession of short-term night watchmen prepared to go off duty one morning, and decided to shave as daylight was breaking. Suddenly, in the mirror, he caught sight of a man behind him, a young sailor, peering over his shoulder. Whirling around, he saw that he was alone. He abandoned his shaving gear, left the ship, and never went back.

Mr. Stewart was fascinated by the bizarre and horrible. He told me that when Poe's wife died, Poe had kept her body in the house —perhaps, he said, in answer to my indelicate question, for weeks, or even months until it was forcibly removed by the police. He told me that John Paul Jones' body was preserved in alcohol in a crypt beneath the chapel at the Naval Academy in Annapolis, and because of its tendency to float upwards, it had to be covered with straw and the alcohol changed or renewed once a year. He told me of a museum somewhere in the Baltimore-Washington area that had all sorts of oddities in it: five-footed chickens, two-headed snakes, even whole people bizarrely mis-formed, all preserved in formaldehyde.

He wondered if I would like to go down to the docks with him and see the *Constellation*. I, though extremely innocent, didn't think that sounded like a very good idea. Daylight was vanishing from the little cemetery; I had studying to do, I said, and prepared to leave. Perhaps another day? He said he was at the ship on Tuesdays and Thursdays …

Ah, but before I left, there was something he wanted to show me. In the now thick twilight of that October afternoon, I allowed myself to be led down the back stairs of the church into the cellar, where he opened a heavy door to the basement. He trained a flashlight into the blackness and my eye, along with the dim beam of light, fell where it glowed.

The darkest reaches I could not see, but the light danced eerily over the strangest sight I had ever beheld: old coffins in messy rows, some caved in, some splintered, some piled atop others and even, here and there, human bones lying white to the musty air, and finally, at long last, his pride: in its crushed coffin, the skeleton of a woman that still had all its, or her, hair, steel-gray, flaring out in crimped profusion from the grinning skull, and below it, the ragged remains of some kind of once-white lacy burial dress. The church had been built so quickly that many of the cemetery's occupants had never even been reinterred.

In horror I fled the place. Mr. Stewart's laughter echoed behind me. I never kept our indefinite appointment to tour the *USS Constellation*.

And looking back, it seems that maybe Poe was there after all, still master of the macabre, still perpetuating in death those elusive qualities of morbidity that so fascinate and horrify his devotees today. How was it that I was the only visitor that day, in the "lonesome October of my most immemorial year"? Was our meeting mere coincidence? A drama performed whenever Mr. Stewart had what he believed was an appreciative audience?

As for me, I have never forgotten that visit, that day when I, all unsuspecting, on the verge of life myself, entered briefly the misty mid-region of death in life—the nonlocal mind, perhaps, of Edgar Allan Poe. And as for Poe, he may only have been having, out of some eternal ennui, a last scornful laugh at some fair-haired blue-eyed descendant of the virginal, stupid, and worldly Lady Rowena of Tremaine. As I had long known, Poe preferred brunettes.

But I was asleep back then, still unaware.

12

Across the Pond: British Stories

In 1993, my then-husband and I traveled as usual to Britain, and because I was involved at the time in writing this book, I just blurted out asking many people we met about ghosts and paranormal events. Not one person denied believing in the unseen when I asked. I read a report in the *London Daily Mail* one morning when I was in London that a survey of many thousands of widows (there are so many more of those than widowers) found that 53% believed they had had contact with their deceased husbands.

A taxi-driver in England named Burt Tiller told me that once, when sick, he was sitting dozing by the fire. He awoke suddenly, and his wife, sitting across in another chair, said, "Are you all right?"

Burt remembers hearing himself say, "Yes. Your mother is coming, with Mark (a friend)." He said he had no idea where his words came from, had no recollection of a dream preceding his remark, nor any sense of why he said it, as he didn't "know" they were coming. He reckoned it was somehow connected with his fever. In only a couple of minutes, the doorbell rang, and in came her mother and Mark, who were not expected. A small thing, but who could explain it?

An English friend, Terrence Montague, once witnessed a wreck on the road leading into a small Cornish coast town. Two cars, two drivers apparently dead. He drove immediately to the police station in the center of town, only to learn that similar reports were frequently made—that nobody knew of an original wreck, but that people reported one all the time at that place, and that whenever the police investigated, there was nothing to be found. Terrence, still unconvinced, drove back the short distance to the site where he had seen the two cars, fronts smashed together, two drivers, each slumped over a steering wheel—and the road was empty.

A friend in Cambridge, England, Lady May Wilson, spoke matter-of-factly about a ghost she had seen "many times" in the fifteenth century house she lived in as a young wife. Her three children saw the figure too, and complained of a lady that woke them up, then stood over their beds crying. The ghost, wringing her hands and weeping, roamed the halls and the children's room.

Lady May was able to research the house's past and learn that three centuries before, a woman living there had lost her three children in a typhoid epidemic. The ghostly woman's clothing and her actions seemed to fit the period of the recorded tragedy.

Lady May, unruffled, acted in recounting this as if *all* houses had ghosts—and why wouldn't the desperate woman be seeking her lost children? They moved away from the house after three years when her husband was transferred—but not because of the ghost!

England is so full of black-dog ghost stories that books have been written on that subject alone—ghostly black dogs that haunt certain roadways, especially cross-roads, all over the island. Large black disappearing dogs are reported at those same places over and over, by people who don't know each other even if they were inclined to invent such stories. Sometimes the dogs are supposed to be harbingers of death.

Those stories resonate with me, because—not in England, but in the flat creek-veined tidewater section of Virginia—I was researching Pocahontas, returning to my motel from a visit to the Pamunkey Reservation one evening in late summer about twilight, when a large black dog ran out of the woods and hit my car head-on. There was a hard thump. I wasn't driving fast, it was a narrow road. Horrified, I pulled over, wanting to check how badly hurt the dog was, could see in my rearview mirror as the dog made its way back into the pinewoods along the country road. I got out of the car and followed the dog, which I would have said was probably a large male black lab. Though the woods were piney, thin forest, I never could find a trace of the dog, alive or dead. With darkness descending swiftly, I had to return to the car and drive on.

Ghost dog? I wouldn't have said so back then. (There's always a more logical explanation, right?) The slight dent over my right front tire was real.

A Cornish cab-driver named Terry drove us and our luggage from Falmouth to Penzance one day. When I asked if he believed in spirits, he said, "Absolutely," and straightaway told us the following story. Just after he was married, three nights in a row he woke to find a man sitting in a deep window in the room he and his bride were occupying in his mother-in-law's house. The man wore shirtsleeves and braces (suspenders), and swung his legs back and forth in an odd way.

Not wanting to alarm his wife (who never awakened), Terry said nothing until after the figure put in its third appearance in as many nights, when he decided to tell not his rather timid wife but his mother-in-law. So he mentioned it cautiously at breakfast before his wife came downstairs.

Immediately his mother-in-law said excitedly, "That's Jack! He used to sit in that window, swinging his legs in just that way!" Jack was her husband and the bride's father, who had been dead for several years, and whom Terry had never met.

The proprietress of *The Lion Inn* where we stayed in Wales, Jean Thomas, told me that when she and her husband first came to Berriew, a small town in Powys near the English border, they lived two years in another cottage before they were able to buy *The Lion*. One room in it from time to time smelled horribly of rotting fish. No cause could be found, and there was no consistency in the manifestation of the disgusting odor. No cleaning affected it, but then it would just vanish abruptly. As it was the spare room, Jean just closed it off and tried to ignore it.

When Jean's sister visited, the occasionally-fishy room was the only one unoccupied, so her sister had to stay in that room. She stayed there only one night, overcome, she claimed, with not only the nasty smell but also an aura, or atmosphere, that was unpleasant and menacing. After that, Jean's sister chose to sleep on the couch in the living room, and did not want to go back into the room, not even in daylight, to collect her things.

Jean discovered that the previous owner, who had died there, did have a fisherman husband who had pre-deceased her. His ashes had been scattered in the garden outside the cottage.

Jean, her husband Brian, and her sister all received the impression that the presence was a male who didn't want strangers in his house, so he apparently repelled them with repulsive odors and unfriendly, evil, energy.

My then-husband and I in 1994 went back to England for a week, then took a boat to France, rented a car, and drove through Normandy and Brittany. The ancient stone monuments at Carnac were our destination, though in between we had no reservations anywhere. I had my usual fat novel that I always take when I travel to read in my spare time—this time A.S. Byatt's *Possession*. I knew it was a sort of modern Victorian novel, set in England where we were going; but I did not know the plot involved anywhere but England. In fact, the action moves not only to the European mainland (where we were also going), but to Brittany, and eventually *to the same town we ended up in.*

In the novel, the main characters rented a red Volkswagen, and were pursued by a black Mercedes. The rental car we were assigned turned out to be a *red Volkswagen*.

Go figure, as my son says.

13

Objects with Minds of their Own

Many people believe objects have life—perhaps a lower form than animals, but life nonetheless. Objects and their owners are often reunited against all probability; in a world as chock-full of objects as ours, it seems there must be something more than mere coincidence. From many incidents of accurate psychometry (reading an object to obtain information about its owner), and from stories such as Kingwood Sprott's finding his long-lost ring, possibly we can conclude that even apparently *inanimate objects have some form of animation or life*. Thousands of cultures, by the way, believe and have believed this, naming certain rocks or trees, certain caves or other natural spots as graced, haunted, or sacred.

For instance, we knew a lawyer who lived in our town awhile with the distinctive name of Kingswood Sprott, Jr. In 1996, after he'd moved back to Florida from Lexington, he was one day forced to crash-land his hot air balloon in a stranger's yard fifty miles or so from his Florida home.

He went to the door, introduced himself to the woman who answered his knock, and apologized for the trespass. The woman looked shocked for a moment, then said, "I have your 1956 Washington and Lee class ring."

She said she'd found it twenty years before on the bottom of Lake Worth in Florida, with his name engraved on it. She'd tried at the time to find Sprott, but he had just moved away from Lake Worth. When she couldn't track him down, she just put the ring in her jewelry box. Not surprisingly, the unusual name of the owner stayed in her mind.

As he waited at her front door, she went to her jewelry box and got the ring and presented it to him. He had swum in Lake Worth about 25 years before—though he had no idea that's where he'd lost his ring. The chances of this coincident meeting and the happy return of his ring seem almost nonexistent. This story made the Associated Press.

In Frankford, West Virginia, Marilyn Carney lost an earring she loved, and put the left single earring away in her jewelry box. They moved miles away, and two years passed. One day the lost earring appeared right in the middle of a made-up bed. Marilyn naturally thought it was the one from her jewelry box, and went to put it back, only to find that one still there. She has never been able to explain how that lost earring returned to her.

At the beach in Mexico, in 2001, a sign at the desk warned us that if we lost our hotel room keys it would cost us *one hundred dollars*. I pointed to the sign, and asked, "Really?"

The female desk clerk looked levelly at me. "Si," she said. So I wore ours around my neck the entire time. But one day, body-surfing, I got tumbled by a wave, and when I got out of the water, my key had disappeared, the cord slipping off at some point in my sea-larking. Of course I went back into the water right away in a futile attempt to find it; but the surge and fall of the waves made for a useless expenditure of energy.

But I decided it *would* return to me. It was, for a few hours, of *primary importance* that it do so. One hundred dollars? No way we were going to pay that. The girl at the desk smiled indulgently when I told her I would find it. She mildly assured me that keys lost in the ocean did *not* return to the same place (it made sense to me that they might, given that waves washed in on the sand continually, bringing seaweed and *other* flotsam in, before pulling back out to sea). I somehow figured I would get our key back, nonetheless. To this day, I'm not clear why. It seemed to have something to do with my determination, my intent, but the odds were clearly against my finding it.

Next morning early, I walked the beach to look for it, and there it was, tossed up for me to find, its black neck cord still attached. It felt as if I had *willed* it back. Coincidence? Maybe. Maybe not. One hundred dollars can be powerful motive, but not *that* powerful!

Beverley Tucker, a Lexington artist, tells of what seemed to her a tale of an evil object. It happened in Sherman, Texas, where she was Dean of Admissions at Austin College. A student she knew mentioned to her one day that he had just bought a house that he thought was haunted. Bev knew the house: Victorian, run-down, surrounded by a wrought-iron fence with an ornate gate out front.

Her student collected antiques; Bev had heard by the grapevine that he got them by cultivating old ladies in the town and spending time with them. At least two grateful women had left him property of value in their wills.

The boy, Byron, told Bev that when he bought the house he already *knew* from dreams before he ever went in every nook and cranny, where every closet was. All his life he had wanted to buy that particular house. He'd come into an inheritance, he told her, and he did buy it.

He invited Bev to come to see the house, which she agreed to do. The arranged evening turned out to be misty, rainy, and spooky, and the gate, when she pushed it open, creaked, just like one might in a horror movie. And she was wearing a black cape that evening.

Byron took her on a tour of the house. In one room on a dresser was an ornate French box with Marie Antoinette figures on it. Bev was drawn to it, and when she examined it, it turned out to be an antique ivory manicure set with little scissors and a buffer and an abrasive file. As she gazed at it, Byron asked, "Do you like that?"

She replied neutrally that it was beautiful, to which Byron said, "I want you to have it. That's why I invited you here. I believe it belonged to you in a past life."

In fact, though she felt that was kind of creepy, Bev felt a strange familiarity with the box, but attributed the feeling to a memory of something in her own past. When Bev had been a little girl, her mother had a similar (though not identical) old-fashioned dresser set, which Bev had been fascinated by. She used to beg her mother to let her play with it.

Byron knew nothing of that. When Byron said he believed it was hers, she had a strong memory of her mother's set, and believes her strange attraction to the box in Byron's house must have come from that association. She didn't know how to respond, and worried about the appropriateness of accepting a valuable gift from someone she didn't know well. She was in her forties, he was in his twenties, and she wondered what it might signal to him if she accepted the gift. She tried to refuse; but in the end he prevailed, insisting that she take the set home with her.

Almost immediately, bad things began to happen to Bev, from minor automobile accidents to plumbing problems to objects falling off shelves, breaking, malfunctioning. From the moment she accepted it, she felt a "knot in her gut" associated with the manicure set. The feeling of menace surrounding it grew.

In a short time, she just had to get rid of it. She put it into her car trunk, reluctant to just toss out such a valuable antique, but not sure what to do with it. She thought about taking it to a pawn shop to be free of it.

She was driving to visit her nephew in Tulsa the next day, and forgot to get rid of the set. On the way she had a blowout. As she took her suitcase from the car trunk in Tulsa, aided by her nephew, she remarked, "I'm getting rid of this thing. It's nothing but trouble. It gave me a blowout coming here today."

But her nephew Mark, eyeing the box, said that if she didn't want it, he would like to keep it. She tried to dissuade him, telling him its history. He insisted he wanted it, and said if it gave him any trouble, he'd just get rid of it.

Once free of it, she put it out of her mind. But when she next saw Mark, she asked him about the box.

"I threw it out," he said. "From the moment I got it, everything in the world started happening to me."

Some time later, Bev tried to locate Byron, the box's original owner, again. She figured he must be rich, for she learned that he'd moved to Fort Worth, and bought an old high-rise, twenty one stories of apartments inhabited by mostly elderly people. He'd decided to turn it into a ritzy condominium, and in doing so evicted many of the people who'd spent years of their lives there. Bev, determined to try to see him, drove to see the condo he'd built out of the old apartment building. To her surprise, she found it boarded up and neglected. Byron wasn't in the phone book, and his venture had obviously failed. The story still haunts her.

14

Oddities

About 1932 several members of my mother's family (then stationed at Quantico) visited a popular Washington psychic of the day. My grandmother went first, and was impressed. So then her daughter, Polly (now 93), went with her then-fiance, Lamar Curry. He had been orphaned at two, and raised by an older sister who told him his father died in a carriage crash—but had protected him from the gruesome details. Mme. McLaren (the psychic) told him his father's death had occurred as the result of having his chest crushed when the carriage ran over him. His sister later confirmed this. Polly witnessed all this.

Polly was told by Mme. McLaren that her future husband should beware of bay horses; that they would have twins born in a foreign country; that she should avoid deep water. She wrote down all these things. She married her fiance, and had three children.

Several years later, Polly's husband got thrown and severely injured by a bay horse. Though Polly never had twins, my mother, her sister Betty, had *two pairs of twins*, one of them born (to die after a few hours) in China. Polly has all her life avoided deep water, though she feels she is a good swimmer.

My mother, Betty, then went down from Annapolis to Washington to visit the psychic with a friend of hers named Laura who had just gotten married; she removed her wedding ring to trick the seer. Laura went in for her sitting first, and Mme. McLaren said, "I can't work with you. Tell my secretary to refund your money." Laura left in a snit, thinking that the psychic had somehow intuited or been told that she was married but pretending to be single.

When my mother went in for her sitting, Mme. McLaren handed her an envelope and told her to put it in her purse, and after two weeks to give it to her friend Laura.

A few days later Laura, apparently desperately unhappy, committed suicide. She had told nobody of her misery. In that emotional time, Mama (Betty) forgot all about the note.

Some weeks later, Mama found the sealed note still in her purse, and opened it. It read, "You have no future."

My friend Skip Davis was down on his luck, had a drinking problem, and many debts. On July 27, 1967, he decided to rob a bank. He explained to me how he'd been wasting money and, in his words, "listening to evil spirits." That July day, in desperation, he went to talk to his brother-in-law, the one person who might have talked him out of his crazy and dangerous plan, but who turned out not to be home. Now Skip knew that his brother-in-law had a gun. Skip stole the gun and his brother-in-law's car, held up a Lexington, Virginia, branch bank, and fled town with the bank bags tossed onto the back seat.

He was stopped five miles south of Lexington at a farmer's market by state troopers who had received the All Points Bulletin on a bank robber, and had set up a road block to catch the thief.

Skip thought—even hoped on some level—that the jig was up. But as his car moved slowly forward in the line for inspection, something distracted the troopers and they absently waved him on by, though he had the gun and what would turn out to be $7,511 in stolen money in bank bags in clear view, and a stolen car.

In Roanoke, he stopped to buy some clothes and a briefcase to put the money in, and kept going. Near Greensboro, North

Carolina, he suddenly felt he *had* to go west to Nashville, where he'd lived several years before. He didn't know why. But he kept going.

When he got to Nashville, he used some of the money to buy a second-hand Cadillac, a guitar and a sequined suit, with the fuzzy intention of becoming a country singer—as he'd always loved to sing. Suddenly a memory from the past overtook him: while they'd lived in Nashville, during a hard time, his wife had hocked her wedding ring at a small store. In a touching act, Skip retrieved the ring with twenty dollars of his ill-gotten gains. Somewhere in this confusing odyssey, he began to pray.

In Nashville, he called his wife long-distance from a phone booth. When he learned from her sister that she'd gone to the drive-in with a girl-friend, he made another call, this time to Sheriff Chittum of Rockbridge County, and told him what he'd done, and said he was coming home. Still not sure why he was doing any of this, he headed back towards Virginia.

Back in Lexington, he drove his brother-in-law's car up to the jail, and turned himself in. That night he prayed while lying on the jail bunk. He told me, "God made a big knot come up on my neck." The entire cell began to glow, so Skip took that for a sign that God heard him praying. Skip then badly wanted an apple and in his prayer asked God for one. Before long, a fellow arrived with, of all things, a bushel of apples for the jail inmates, and he got one. The knot on his neck went down after he ate the apple. He continued to pray.

Subsequently, the bank auctioned off the Cadillac bought with stolen money, the sequined suit, and the guitar—which brought in more money than Skip had stolen. Because his conversion was so obviously real to his jailers, he was given the balance of the money after the bank had gotten back its money. He presented his wife with her hocked wedding ring.

Skip gives God all the credit for setting him straight, protecting him throughout, and fixing absolutely everything, even down to the return of the little silver wedding band. Though the accoutrements of his dream ambition were auctioned off, Skip has gone on to found a church, become its preacher, sing gospel songs to his congregation, learning to play the guitar as he went along. Today he has a commercial CD, and "with God's help" has become the gospel singer he'd dreamed of being. Skip believes the entire, rather loopy, episode was set up by God, or God's angels, to save his soul.

The way I came to know Skip is that I read one day in the fall of 1967 about the auction of the car, the costume, and guitar, and was so intrigued by the story I visited him in jail, and subsequently used his story as a subplot in a novel I was writing. We were friends from them on. He dropped by from time to time to say hello, and was always tickled that I'd portrayed him in my first novel, *I Will Go Barefoot All Summer for You*.

Toni Williams of Natural Bridge had two friends in graduate school who "made contact" via Ouija board sessions with a man calling himself, let's say, "Boyd Fishwick."

One day the Ouija board spelled out the message, *Beware. Boyd Fishwick lives.* They were somewhat freaked out, but unsure what to do; they finally took the high ground that Boyd Fishwick was just a silly invention of their own minds.

Later that day, in their car, they suddenly drove around a bend to find a car stopped sideways across the road, too close for them to avoid. Fortunately, they were not going fast and nobody was badly hurt in the crash that ensued. The other driver's name was, incredibly, Boyd Fishwick.

A man named Henry Fleury did odd jobs for us for years. He was deeply religious—and seemed fascinated with the fact that we were without religion. He actually said once that we were "such good people," that he couldn't believe we weren't Christian. I always had the feeling that he was trying to figure us out. In Henry's presence, we had some odd occurrences. Though this may not be the case, I associated the strangeness with his faith.

One time when my ex-husband and I were in the woods (he looked for birds while I looked for mushrooms), he was using some expensive binoculars I'd bought him for Christmas. When we got back to the car the binoculars were not in his pocket. We were both distressed; but we'd been tramping all over the mountainside, and there was no sense in going back to look for them in the pathless, brushy forest. We both knew he had them in the woods; and both of us looked all around and searched the Jeep. Then we came home.

Four months passed. One day Henry was working for us at our house in the country, when he handed my husband the binoculars. Henry said he'd found them on the floor of the back seat of my husband's Jeep. To us, that seemed impossible. They'd been lost in the woods. We had searched the car thoroughly, more than once. We never had any explanation for the return of the binoculars.

On another occasion, my husband's wallet vanished. He scoured his office and the house and his car, looking everywhere. Our cleaning lady, Adeline Suthers, (Addie), went over the house every Thursday, but never found it. Weeks passed.

There was a leak one day around the base of the toilet in his office, so we called Henry to come work on it. Henry obliged him, and when he came out of the bathroom he handed my husband his lost wallet, saying he'd found it *behind the toilet*. My husband again felt that was impossible, insisting that that was the *first* place he'd looked. Addie had cleaned the bathroom every week. To this day, we don't understand the wallet's mysterious return. Nothing was missing.

Clyde Beck has an English friend Trudy Brown, who together with her husband owned a chain of laundromats in Germany. Trudy, discouraged and depressed following her husband's untimely death, put the laundromats on the market. To cheer her up, a friend persuaded her to visit a psychic, asking for a message from her husband with something verifiable that could let her know it really was him.

The psychic first gave her a message: "I love the shoes." At first Trudy couldn't connect that comment to her husband at all, then remembered she had bought him some shoes some time before, which he hadn't worn much. She prayed for a more definite message.

Suddenly, as she did, the psychic said, "Keep on with the washing." Keep on with the washing? It took a bit, but then she realized that the message clearly was not to sell the laundromat chain. So she changed her plans, and kept them, and they have made her a wealthy woman today.

Clyde also tells me he was physically attacked by gnarled, angry, diminutive elves as he slept on the floor of a house he was building that had just gone "under roof" on Angel Island in Montana. Another carpenter slept on another pallet across the room. Beck described the elves as wearing only loin cloths, and looking like "old babies" about twenty inches tall. They were strong, strangling him, preventing his breathing, and it seemed clear to Clyde that they were trying to kill him, and might succeed.

Finally, he gasped, "In the name of Jesus, leave me alone!" and they stopped, releasing the hold they had on him, backed off, and vanished. He says his expletive was just that, and not an honest prayer. Clyde thinks the elves were trying to kill him for invading and building on what they considered their land. Clyde answered, at my question, that he was awake, sober, and drug-free, when this happened. Later in a book by G. Manley Hall about gnomes, gremlins, and other such creatures, Clyde saw a picture of what his attackers looked like.

Since they vanished, I would put them in the ghostly category, though their attack seemed physical. Clyde thinks they may have been "elementals," whose home he was inadvertently destroying by building a house in that lovely wilderness.

I asked if he had been able to do anything to placate the little guys after that frightening attack, but he said he could not, though the place later became a ghost town. Clyde had no money, and was merely the construction foreman with no power to stop work on the project.

Perhaps the creatures realized that Beck was not responsible, for they never returned to menace him again. It was in a mining area, near the Sarco gold and silver mines—and the Anaconda lead mines, which were polluting the area, and eventually caused its abandonment—perhaps the little people in the end had their way.

Clyde has seen many UFO's over his remote Highland County farm, and years ago took me to a totally bare spot of burnt grass halfway up a rocky mountain. He said a UFO had landed there several years before, and stayed several hours, lighting up the night sky. I've been to the spot many times since, and it's always barren, no matter the season.

Clyde, despite his many odd experiences, still believed there was nothing after death until he had an experience that changed his life forever. He had a friend named Frank who'd been a pilot in Vietnam, and had suffered severe mental problems since. Only seventeen years after the war was over, when he was 42, could Frank function again. At that time he came to work half-time as a carpenter with Clyde, who was sympathetic about his difficulties. Frank continued to go twice a week into Washington to see a psychiatrist.

Two days before Thanksgiving one year, Frank told Clyde he wanted to take off a few days to visit his children because he had a fear that he would not reach his forty-third birthday. Clyde, always understanding, agreed to let him off work.

But the day after Thanksgiving, there was a large plane crash in Loudon County, Virginia, and Clyde, head of a citizens' group, became part of the grisly job of cleanup. He had no choice but to call Frank to come help.

"Would I have to see dead people?" Frank wanted to know.

Clyde said that was unavoidable; so Frank said he was sorry, but he could not help. That puzzled Clyde, for Frank had seen plenty of death in Vietnam.

Two days later, Frank's wife called Clyde to say that Frank had died suddenly in his sleep.

On the third day after Frank's death, Clyde had just turned out his light for the night, when he perceived Frank standing by his bed, looking just as he had in life. Frank, Clyde swears, touched him physically on the shoulder, and said, "Everything's going to be all right," and vanished. Clyde from that moment on has known that the human spirit survives death, and believes that Frank's post-death visit was specifically to make him understand that.

Barbara Geddes, a housemother at our local Phi Gamma Delta fraternity, had a long-time relationship with a man she loved. At the time of this occurrence, she knew he was near death. Early one morning, she had a dream that he came to her, and said insistently, "Come with me. Come on." He took her by her arm, and half pulled her *out of her body*. She found herself sitting up, and could look back at her sleeping form on the bed still connected at waist level.

She said to him, "No, this isn't my time. I can't come with you." She felt the snap of separation, and he disappeared. Later that morning she learned that he had died at the time she had her experience, or dream. She has sometimes felt his presence since, and knows he is waiting for her on the other side of death.

On April 1, 2001, *The Roanoke Times* reported on the sad life and death of a homeless alcoholic man named David Goodman. His mother had not heard from him for many months when he died. She had taken him as a foster child when he was six or seven, but their relationship had been a failure more or less from the beginning. At ten, he was already an alcoholic. His life had been ruined by alcohol. He had spent time in prison, and only called his foster mother occasionally, usually late at night, when he needed to beg her for money.

Policemen came to her door to describe how he had been hit and killed on Orange Avenue in Roanoke as he attempted to crawl across the street.

Mrs. Goodman, heartsick even though their relationship had been one of sadness and estrangement, decided to cancel a trip she had planned to St. Martin. But friends urged her to go ahead, pointing out that there was nothing she could do to change anything by staying in Roanoke. David was dead.

In the three days since she'd heard of his death, she had not been able to sleep. Reluctant and exhausted, she allowed herself to be persuaded, and boarded her plane, where she immediately fell into a deep sleep. She dreamed that David, bathed in warm light, approached her, looking not haggard and ill as he had the last time she'd seen him, but "cherubic," as he had been as an appealing foster child.

I quote from the *Times* article written by Zeke Barlow:

"David, David, David," Goodman cried as her son came near.

"It's all right, Mom, it's all right. I'm okay now." He repeated, "I'm sorry. I'm sorry."

"David, don't say you're sorry," she said just before he faded away. "It's enough to know that you are all right now."

My older brother, John Letcher, was teaching physics at a university on the west coast when a student answered every single question on a graduate exam with precisely the same wording and figuring that my brother had done in working through his own exam. The answer sheet had not been out of Johnny's possession since he'd made up the exam. There was no way that anyone could have so perfectly mimicked his equations and his conclusions. He felt he had no choice but to call the student in and question him about how he reached his answers.

The student looked horrified, and said that this was not the first time he'd had this sort of thing happen. As far as he knew, he was just answering the questions the exam asked, but he'd been confronted by the same kind of suspicions before. Johnny, being of a scientific and thoughtful nature, pondered the problem, came again and again to realize that the student had *no way* of physically seeing the exam. He finally concluded that the boy had somehow traveled out of body and seen the exam before taking it, and absolutely had no intentions of cheating, as well as *no way to cheat*—at least on the material plane. He gave the boy an A, as his answers were perfect.

My niece Lucy Letcher of Southwest Harbor, Maine, Johnny's oldest daughter, says she often decides at night what she wants to dream about, then is able to do so. What an enviable gift! She was sailing with the rest of her family on the inland waterway to Alaska one summer, and she decided she wanted in her dream to see a bear—then amended her intent to include, *at a safe distance*.

That night she dreamed she and her two sisters were walking on a sandy beach without their parents. When she looked behind, she saw bear tracks on the sand behind them alongside their own footprints, where there had been none as they walked down the beach. She woke disappointed not to have had "her dream."

The next day, while anchored in shallow water, their parents told the girls to go on shore for awhile in the skiff. Lucy said *No*, remembering her dream.

"All right," said their mother, "Susan and Alice can go on by themselves." At that, Lucy knew that as the oldest, she had to go too, as she was sure they would encounter the bear.

On the beach, the dream scene was indeed repeated, with a

few differences: for example, the beach, which had been sand in her dream, was now rock, so she was relieved.

But in fact, a grizzly came out of the bushes, and started towards the three sisters.

Susan ran towards her sisters, throwing rocks at the bear and screaming. They all ran back to the skiff, fortunately—because the skiff had just unlodged itself and was floating away out to sea. They had not pulled it onto the beach securely enough.

All three girls ran screaming into the water, caught the skiff, clambered in, and returned to the boat. Susan recalls that Lucy kept saying, "I knew it. I knew it. I knew we were going to see a grizzly."

Vision? Dream? Rosalie Stewart Detch of Lewisburg, West Virginia (a student at one of my Elderhostels), owned a motel. Some years back, she hired a fellow to work for her. From the beginning something, she thought, was odd about him, yet familiar. Try as she might, she could not figure out what it was. Soon after he came to work for her, she had a vision—not a dream, she emphasizes—in which it seemed that the man was related to her, probably a brother, and that they were children together, in another time, running, in wooden shoes, along a cobbled street, with a huge fire behind them. Other people were on the street, too, and there was a sense of excitement and urgency. She feels they were in some place "such as Denmark."

As they ran, there in front of them was "the oddest cart I ever saw." It was huge and wooden, and had enormous wooden wheels.

One night soon after this vision, Rosalie awoke with a dreadful pain in her leg, and knew somehow that the pain belonged to the strange man working for her. In fact, he had at the exact time she awakened, suffered an automobile accident, injuring his leg.

Later, the man ran off with another motel employee; but before he did, Rosalie mentioned these strange episodes to the man. He did not in any way share her sense of familiarity or respond to any of the details of a past life together that her vision seemed to suggest. Her sympathetic pain concerning his injured leg meant nothing to him.

The episode was unsettling to Rosalie, and so she prayed about it. She asked for a sign that it was a true vision representing a past life, and not "just her imagination." In fact, she asked God to send her a *wooden shoe* as a sign, if her vision was true.

Several months later, Rosalie and her husband were on a vacation when she hurt her foot and couldn't walk on it. She found an orthopedic surgeon to treat the foot. He examined her, then told his nurse, "Get the medium wooden shoe."

Rosalie recalled her prayer for a sign, and believes, therefore, that what happened to her is at least in some sense *real*.

From these stories I conclude that perhaps in that mysterious realm where we go after death, we finally are able to be *who we think we are*, or *who we want to be*. Recall Celia Green's words that after death, apparently people can change at will and look the way (and the age) they want to. Almost everyone who visits that realm and returns—that is, those who experience near-death events—report the same thing: healthy, splendid-looking people, persons they have known only when old whose youth has been restored, and some, like Addie's husband, whose looks have changed entirely, yet are clearly themselves. People visiting the realms beyond death report that most people they meet there seem to be generally somewhere around 35. In *Coming Back*, Raymond Moody tells of an encounter with a young woman he did not at first recognize. Later he realized that the woman, who appeared to be a stranger, was his grandmother, whom he had known only when she was very old.

When I had the visit with my grandfather, I noted his wispy. white hair, though his face seemed broader and less lined than I recall. I have pondered that: my Andaddy was the *youngest* son of Virginia's Civil War governor John Letcher, and was a great civic leader in his own life (1872-1954)—a time when some age was deemed beneficial to a man. It's been suggested that the reason so many young Civil War officers wore beards was to appear older than they were, and thus more mature and worthy to lead. Thus perhaps my grandfather chooses in the Afterlife to appear *older* than the average thirtyish looking person on the other side.

David McKnight described to me once the experience that made a believer out of him. It was 1969, David was living in New York, and was asked to sit in on a seance whose purpose was to try to contact the dead son of a couple, both Columbia professors. They were deeply grieving the loss of their child. David was told nothing except that their son had died in his twenties. David got no information that he could pass along to the grieving parents; in fact, throughout the seance he had a kinesthetic experience, a sensation in his own body of rolling and dizziness, which he attributed at the time to his own stress. So he kept quiet.

At the end of the seance, after the professors had left, David asked the leader how the son had died. The young man had either jumped or fallen down a steep hill from a rapidly moving train. For David the experience was unique, inexplicable in logical terms, and eventually he could reach no conclusion but that his feeling was a real contact from the young man on the other side.

If only we could easily access that open channel to whatever it is we need to know! My first cousin John Curry (older son of Aunt Polly), now a physician, entered the high school cafeteria in Evanston, Illinois, one day in the fifties when he was a student there, and sat down next to two boys he did not know well and had no classes with—who were discussing spelling. He interrupted them, saying, "Wait just a minute. Give me some paper." One of the boys handed him a torn piece of paper, and John wrote something on it, folded it tightly and set it on the table between them. "Go on with your conversation," John said.

"Well," one boy went on, "I bet you can't spell this word I learned today. Mnemonic." Of course the other boy started with "n," then guessed "pn," and "gn," and finally gave up. The first boy finally told him how to spell it.

John then indicated the paper lying still folded between them on the table. On it he had impulsively written the word, "mnemonic." He doesn't know to this day why or how he did it. He had no classes with the other boys, and hardly knew them.

Today, years later, he shakes his bald head remembering, and says philosophically, "Ah. Now. The *real* trick is to figure out how to do it again!"

I had one such experience myself, maybe fifteen years ago. Upon seeing some map coordinates, the words "St. Louis Arch" flew out of my mouth. That turned out to be the correct location of the numbers. I most certainly did not know that in any sense that I understand "knowing," and felt surprised and somewhat embarrassed at the flurry of awed reactions that followed. I had no explanation. Still don't.

Shortly after my separation from my ex-husband, a man came to interview me for a magazine. I at once "saw" him as a monk; I had no idea why, except that his hair was a monkish fringe. But so is the hair of many bald men. In fact, that was my secret moniker for him, way before I got to know him, "the monk." He was in fact a jazz musician, and I soon forgot my original impression. But I'd made a note of it the day we met. In fact, within six weeks I knew that my "instant snapshot" of him as a monk was 100% correct. He was celibate and religious and contemplative. I have to conclude that intelligence contains more than logic and material information.

My brother Johnny believes he was abducted by aliens around 1973. One morning, John, his wife Pati, and Pati's sister Pegi, gathered for breakfast. They all shared a feeling of having had a strangely unquiet night. In the early morning hours, there was a loud bang; everyone agreed they'd heard it, and all were awakened by it. They all had seen a lot of blue and orange lights blinking in their eyes. When Johnny went to look out the window, "I saw what seemed to be a bright turbulent column of light over the pond, that faded and disappeared over a space of about ten seconds." They all felt "zapped" for the rest of the day. Next day Johnny went to investigate what he had decided must have been a shot hitting an electric transformer, rupturing it and causing electrical arcing and meltdown. He was surprised to find no damage to the street lights at all, no scorching, short circuit, or anything at all out of order. He also looked at the side of their house for a bullet hole, feeling he could then make an official complaint. But he found nothing.

A day or two later, Johnny had a sore in his right nostril, and when he mentioned it to his wife, he learned that she had one too. So, it turned out, did his wife's sister, and so had their father. Worried that the old house might have an infestation of infective spores of some kind, he asked his physician father-in-law about it, but Dr. Ryan seemed unconcerned. The sores all healed in a few days.

That's where it ended at the time. Johnny and Pati would discuss it from time to time. "Do you remember that night when we woke to that bang, and there were all those colored lights?" And they'd confirm their memories of it, and wonder about it. Johnny is a scientist, and it was so strange and inexplicable that he felt embarrassed to bring it up lest people find him, in his own words, "even odder than I already am."

Around 1988 Johnny came upon *Abduction*, by John Mack. As he read it, skeptical about the entire topic, immediately it started making him panicky and nervous, and raising the hair on the back of his neck. There he found one account after another of similar experiences to his: an unquiet night, a loud bang, colored lights outside, sore noses.

Johnny wrote to Dr. Mack, and received a warm invitation to come to Cambridge and undergo hypnosis. As he made plans to go, Johnny explains how he began to feel he was "being told not to go." Though curious, Johnny was unable to actually bring himself to dial Mack's number. *Something* prevented him.

At the time he was in contact with Dr. Mack, he asked Pati again what she recalled of the experience. She asked him what in the world he was talking about, denied any recollection at all of the events, or of their ever talking about it afterwards. Johnny quickly called Dr. Ryan, who also claimed no memory whatsoever of the events. Sister Pegi also remembered nothing.

Johnny would still like to go see Dr. Mack, though he has a deep fear of hypnosis. He recalls that Mack would follow up, call and express disappointment that Johnny was reluctant to come, but understanding too. Johnny thinks he recalls that his reluctance was a pattern Mack acknowledged seeing before. And the meeting between them never happened. And Mack, of course, is dead now.

To this day, whenever I bring it up, my brother says he feels a strong compunction *not to talk about it*. As far as he knows, he's never had another encounter. My brother's IQ is at the genius level, he is a member of Mensa, and it makes sense to me that he might well be chosen for communication by more advanced intelligences than ours. It even seems strange to *him* that he's not more motivated to investigate what happened, for as an aeronautical engineer he is trained to pursue strange phenomena. He feels he should be able to "look this thing in the face." But he admits he can't. Bowing out of the experience, backing away, seems to be a common connection with abductees. (Dr. Mack died tragically a few years ago, run down by a taxi in London.)

On March 22, 1982, an overcast night in the panhandle of West Virginia, Donn (Buddy) Shallcross of Augusta, just across the state border from Winchester, Virginia, thought he saw a small plane go down as he arrived home around 4 a.m. from his job as an emergency medical technician. He drove as close as he could to the scene, where his car inexplicably stopped. Shallcross then took a flashlight to light his way across a fence and into a field of high grass.

He was swinging the light back and forth, when it shone on a telephone pole—and a pair of legs. He guessed it was a person from the plane, and asked, "Are you all right?"

There was no response to his question, repeated several times, so he said, "Who are you?" It appeared to be a person about 5'6" tall, standing with military erectness in a one-piece, silver, skin-tight uniform with a visor covering his eyes, and an object that Shallcross described as a cylinder roughly the size of a baseball bat.

"I am a watch guard," the person replied.

"Where are you from?" Shallcross asked, still with the plane crash scenario playing out in his mind.

"I am not from here," the figure replied tersely.

"Have you been here before?" Donn asked.

"Many times."

"The same ones?" (I quote from the original transcript. Shallcross does not know why he asked this.)

"Others also."

"Why haven't you made yourselves known?"

"We are known," was the curt reply.

As the conversation continued, sometimes verbal but mostly telepathic, Shallcross got the idea that the person and his people were concerned with disposal of atomic waste and its polluting effects.

Suddenly, but without moving, Shallcross and the figure were standing farther into the field, at the base of the craft. Shallcross emphasizes he did not walk there, and the other figure never moved a muscle. The craft, like two soup bowls with the lips pressed together, was about 25 feet across and was hovering about ten feet above the ground. It had a band of lights around the center. As they approached, a ramp opened, and a hazy purple light poured out, bathing Shallcross's face and hands. Immediately he felt uncomfortably hot.

Telepathically, the figure projected images and signs that it indicated Shallcross could use to find the answers to his questions. It also communicated that "they" too acknowledged God. Eventually the figure said it had to leave, but would be back to teach Shallcross more.

In an instant, the figure had disappeared—leaving Shallcross to wonder later if it might not have been a photographic projection of some sort. The hatch or door of the saucer closed, the band around the center began to light up with alternating red and amber lights, and the craft, now humming, started slowly up, getting brighter as it rose above the mountain range—and disappeared.

Shallcross was afterwards able to confirm that two more people had called the state police that night, each believing a plane had crashed, and more than one neighbor later told Shallcross that, sometime during the forty minutes or so he had been in the field, a police officer was heard to say on a scanner, "My God, you won't believe what I see." But the next day when Shallcross went back with a state trooper, they could find nothing.

In the hours following the event, Shallcross developed a terrible burn on his hands and face, and had an upset stomach. Fear might have brought on the nausea, but not the burns. The trooper later confirmed that Shallcross's hands and face were badly burned, and observed that he seemed genuinely frightened.

Being a rational person, Donn had to think long and hard about whether to go public with his story, knowing that he would, henceforth, be seen as one of those "nuts who saw saucers." His decision to do so, of course propelled his life forward in ways he could not have imagined before.

Subsequently, he tried to invite another encounter, but unsuccessfully. A craft returned one night and shined a spotlight down on him and his family for some seconds; but it could not be enticed to land.

Now, twenty years later, Shallcross tells me that before this event, he was not a well-educated man. But since the encounter he has gotten into building and building design, held political office, been a school board member, and narrowly missed winning the mayoral race of his city—without additional education—all of which, he says, would have been unthinkable before his contact.

He has slowly recalled that the alien told or conveyed to him many things that night, including a reference that appeared to be to Itzamna, a mysterious Mayan god which some archaeologists have also connected with Egypt. Shallcross has discovered that virtually all of the world's pyramids are in a rough line running from "ten degrees south of thirty degrees from the equator, to ten degrees north of thirty degrees"—though the meaning of that fact eludes him (as it does me). He believes all pyramids originally generated energy of some sort, and that there is certainly a connection between the pyramids of the new world and the old.

Shallcross, though a modest man, says that his intelligence has been enhanced since his encounter. When pressed to reveal any intellectual or psychological changes since the event, he admits that he now has a near-photographic recall of things as well as a deep interest in esoteric and scientific subjects of many sorts.

A late note: after sending me a huge box of material relating to his encounter, which I read and promptly returned to him, and after several very cordial phone conversations in March of 2002, and a dozen e-mails, Shallcross suddenly ceased communicating with me. Half a dozen e-mails on my part failed to elicit a response. I cannot but wonder if Donn Shallcross could be under the same kind of compulsion that my brother Johnny feels, not to talk about these matters.

Natalie Chadwick grew up in Nottingham, Pennsylvania, and recalls a chilling story that happened when her son, now 23, was not quite two. One night she and her little boy watched a white light like a star that suddenly blew up into a big yellow light. As they watched, her child suddenly said, "We got blood. They don't have blood but we got blood." Her son had nightmares as a child, and one night when he was nine, he crawled into her room one night crying, "They're here! There they are!" She ran into his room, but all seemed fine. In the middle of the floor lay a kitchen spoon.

"What are you doing with a spoon?" Natalie asked.

"The alien with suction cup fingers asked me for one," Justin said. The next morning there were three round dots on the window Justin said the alien left by.

Natalie has always been "open" to psychic phenomena, and the way I met her was that her license plate reads UFO-TRKR. I saw her sitting in her car at the post office, went over, introduced myself, and asked her about it. We talked a week later. She grew up in log cabin house first built in 1714, where she was always aware of a ghostly presence, particularly in one bedroom. When Natalie had to live in that bedroom, she would never hang a mirror, for she was sure if she did, she would see something. She moved to Rockbridge County ten years ago.

I have a friend Lee who swears she was abducted by two kinds of aliens, the "short grays" and "tall, shiny beings"—whom she perceived as superior to the grays—from the time she was an infant until she was 35 (in 1989). Lee feels that finally at about 35, she was rejected from the aliens' program that she'd been "enrolled" in. Her part in the program seems to have been to react to video-like pictures so that the aliens could study (her) human emotional responses. Lee's stories are complex and many-layered, and yet she is as sane as anyone I know.

I asked Lee once if she had any "material proof" of her stories, and she said no—though the aliens had continually promised to leave her something concrete. The only possible evidence of their long association is a paper she still has from her sixth grade science class (I have not seen it) sometime in the sixties, on which she'd drawn Neptune rotating on its side with a thin twisted ring around it. She had learned about astronomy, she told me, from the aliens. The teacher had marked Neptune wrong, and she'd argued with the teacher that she knew she was right. It wasn't until the Voyager 2 visit on August 25, 1989, when Lee was in her thirties, and a biology teacher herself, that scientists discovered that Neptune looked just the way she had drawn it a quarter of a century before.

15

Predictions and Pitfalls

Whatever the prophetic glimpses of the future are, they suggest that sometimes we cannot only see the future, but even change it. The logical conclusion is *that time and inevitability are not what we currently think they are.* I have collected several anecdotes of people seeing or dreaming events before they occurred.

When Barbara Goldsten was a child, her aunt told her a story that had happened to her when *she* was a child. One day she (the aunt) looked up from playing, and said to her mother calmly, "Mrs. Chestnut's house is going to burn down."

The child's mother said, "Oh, dear, what a terrible thing to say! Don't say things like that!"

That night, Mrs. Chestnut's house burned down. The child had somehow known hours before it happened.

While visiting her parents in Alabama one day, Barbara remarked to them, "Isn't it sad about Einstein?"

"What?" her parents wanted to know.

"Well, he died," she said, puzzled at their not knowing.

"No, he didn't," they both said.

Barbara was sure he had, had no idea how she "knew," and looked for it on the evening news. Nothing. The same the next day. But on the third day, the networks were full of the death of Einstein. She had "known" it before it happened.

Charlotte Morgan, a writer and a close friend of mine, recalled a vivid dream she had early one morning when her daughter Miranda was about eighteen months old. The child's crib was in the corner of a room, between two windows. In Charlotte's dream, the child had managed to crawl out of the crib and onto one of the window sills, where she pushed out the screen and fell two floors to the ground— whereupon Charlotte awakened horrified. Immediately she told her husband the terrifying dream.

That afternoon while Miranda napped Charlotte was walking upstairs to check on the child, when she heard her husband yelling her name from outside the house. She followed his voice into the baby's room, where Miranda had crawled onto the window sill, and in fact had pushed the screen out. Husband John, below, was poised to try to catch the child when she fell. Charlotte was able to dart across the room and grab her back to safety. What possible explanation could account for this dream in terms of time as we now understand it?

Jean St. Pierre, a counselor for people who are at mid-point looking for new jobs since the tragic events of September 11, 2001, told me of a dream she had the following January. She was in a misty room with an empty coffin. Her *mother* stood on the other side of it from her. "Is this yours?" Jean asked.

Her mother replied, "No, it's Grandma's."

On *Mother's Day* Jean's grandmother, previously healthy, suddenly died. Jean feels she got the message, quite specific as to time, beforehand.

If even one prediction has ever come true, it argues that *time is not linear*, which in turn argues that *we do not have the slightest idea what time is.*

Many people have reported to me knowing before confirmation

that a daughter was pregnant, or of intuiting the sex of an unborn child (in that case, of course, you're going to be fifty percent right either way!). One woman told me of knowing thirty years ahead of the event that a particular illness would lead to her husband's death—as it did.

However, in my search for information on paranormal events, predictions of important events lose out. I have been unable to prove a single incidence of a clear prediction of a "large event" followed by the event actually happening. I have kept careful files on famous psychics' annual predictions in *Parade* magazine since 1963. I own several books full of predictions for the future. *Not a single prediction that I have on file has ever come true.* And I cannot find on the Internet any report of anyone accurately (or even nearly) predicting the terrorist attacks of September 11, 2001, an event that most of us would agree was of enormous import to the nation, and the planetary society. In some ways, it has changed the world forever.

I own a book about Nostradamus written in 1941 by Lee McCann, which explains the *amazing* accuracy of his predictions all the way up to World War II. The last chapter purports to make predictions for the future (beyond 1941), based on interpreting Nostradamus' further verses. Not one of the future predictions has come to pass. "In 1987, all books will be censored and the offending ones destroyed," according to McCann's interpretation. On August 18, 1999, the "orgy of mankind …will lead to the final date on this earth." Nostradamus vaguely predicted "the rise of the Orient" in the twentieth century, the last quarter of the century full of "shaking, wars, and battles. But by the end of the [twentieth] century there will begin between God and man a universal peace for a thousand years." Needless to say, not one of the predictions beyond 1941 has come true—or been interpreted accurately. A 1995 reinterpretation of Nostradamus claimed that six nuclear power plants would explode in 1996 and 1997, killing thousands immediately, and millions eventually. There were five other doomsday predictions, none of which came to pass. From another book on Nostradamus published in 1999 by Ned Halley: just for example, for the year 2000 Nostradamus predicted nuclear war in Asia, the start of a 40-year drought to be followed by a 40-year flood, and a devastating explosion of a nuclear plant near Bordeaux.

Even Edgar Cayce in this regard has feet of clay. Cayce on June 28, 1940, said, while sleeping, "Poseidia will be among the first portions of Atlantis to rise again. Expect it in '68 and '69—not so far away!" The year 1998, he claimed, would be when there was to be "the change in the earth's position." There's lots more, but none of it is correct.

The unjustifiably famous Jeanne Dixon foresaw in December 1963 "peace at the end of the [twentieth] century," the replacement of Castro by a Russian, and an attack on the United States by Russia with "an ultimate weapon." In 1972, still with a devastating record of wrong predictions, Dixon predicted public office for Dr. Benjamin Spock, and a medical breakthrough that year leading to a cure for cancer.

Another famous (but equally unreliable) psychic, Taylor Caldwell, predicted in 1967 that *before 1970*, "America will be in a major war, probably World War III, a nuclear war." "America is in grave financial shape..." and "the dollar will have to be devaluated," and finished with "cancer will finally be admitted as mildly contagious."

Self-proclaimed psychic David Hoy, in December of 1977 predicted that "Tremendous oil finds in Mexico will be pumped with the United States' technology, and will vastly improve the US economy."

In 1969 scores of psychics got on the bandwagon to predict imminent doomsday in the Golden State of California, including 15 million deaths, and the total destruction of San Francisco.

"Priests will soon be allowed to marry," wrote seeress "Countess Amaya" in June 1972, whose past predictions, so she claimed, had *never* missed. All of her future predictions, however, did miss, including that Puerto Rico would attain statehood in the near future, and that Elizabeth Taylor would soon die.

Kuo, a Chinese seer, in February 1976, predicted that Nelson Rockefeller would become president—and a long list of other things that also did not occur.

Were there any verifiable predictions about September 11, 2001? If so, I never saw, heard, or read of them but one, the story of a fifth grader in Dallas, Texas, who on September 10 casually told his teacher that World War III would begin the next day—and that the United States would lose. This story was reported a week *later* in the Houston *Chronicle*. Osama bin Laden claimed later that there had been many predictive dreams among his followers, but anyone can belatedly claim to have made a prediction earlier.

I do not understand why small predictions seem often to come true, while "big" ones do not. I would urge the institution of a hotline for predictions, which would no doubt get a lot of wrong information, but would also fairly quickly prove if predictions ever do come true, even if they are about mere trivial events.

Until then, I suggest that if your cousin calls to say she dreamed you're having a girl, believe it. But it appears that the way to accurately predict future world-events and the lives of the famous—is to read the psychic predictions, then assume that the exact opposite will occur!

16

Conclusion: As Present As Possible

When I once complained years ago to David McKnight that I had never had a psychic experience, David look astonished, and said, "You have them all the time. Every minute. But you know, even if you had an absolutely convincing one, you'd probably still figure out a way to explain it in the way of the skeptic."

That remark made me rethink events in my own life enough to be able to finish this book. I have progressed, slowly, from total skeptic to the awareness that I indeed do have psychic experiences. I believe we all do, that psychic experience is a part of the human experience as much as seeing and breathing. Some of us ignore the gentle nudgings of spirit, so they aren't a part of our experience. Some of us never see because we disbelieve, and thus "reframe" them into something else. Some of us pay close attention. I've been all three places.

Despite all the stories involving my family, my siblings—my ancestors, the family as a whole remains skeptical. How can that be? Are we all so good at denial that for all of us, our "scientific" beliefs (nothing you can't "prove" exists) forced us to forget later that those "strange" things happened? Was it too much for my father to contemplate, that single predictive dream?

One conclusion I am personally forced to is that *the human soul—and indeed, animal souls, survive bodily death, and on occasion, interact with the living.* Though this may come as no surprise to many of my readers, it did come as a surprise to me.

I first visited the Monroe Institute in 1991. The next year I took a ghost-hunting course, and immediately was recruited into a group of ghost hunters. Several times a year, we visited and de-haunted houses in the area from then until 2004, when David McKnight, our leader, moved to Canada. My next book is about those experiences, as well as my subsequent experiences at the Monroe, where I still go about twice a year for programs, and in the world. The next book is more like a practical guide for communicating across time, about talking with the dead. It will be out about a year from now.

I was a longtime subscriber to a magazine called *The Zetetic* (later *The Skeptical Inquirer*). Its editor, Paul Kurtz, stated without apology the magazine's intent to "pursue paranormal claims mercilessly." It attacked UFO's and spoonbenders, angels, ghost-seers and prophets, with equal vengeance, implying that anyone who believed that stuff was nuts. Kurtz, speaking to *Time* in December of 1977, said, " … once irrationality grows it will spill over into other areas. There is no guarantee that a society so infected by unreason will be resistant to even the most virulent programs of dangerous ideological sects."

I loved *The Skeptical Inquirer*. But it seemed to me picky about details that could not be proven, but were anecdotally repeated over and over (such as abduction claims and ghost sightings); and they resorted to name-calling and sarcasm when they couldn't *logically* disprove something. I cringed at their lofty moralizing. If they couldn't disprove UFO's, they could damn believers as stupid and naive. In a *Smithsonian* article, Kendrick Frazier, one of the editors, defined paranormal as "UFO's, psychics …and other nonsense, including anything not yet experimentally validated."

In 1993 I began subscribing to the British *Paranormal Review* and *The Journal of the Society for Psychical Research*. They came monthly along with the *Skeptical Inquirer*, and for a long time I took all three magazines. Eventually I stopped subscribing to the *Skeptical Inquirer*. Despite its claims, the magazine is *not* open-minded; it is convinced that any paranormal event is a hoax, a mistake, a "dream," headlights, a delusion, swamp gas, hysteria.

As things stand now, skeptics insist that anomalous events be tested by statistical analysis, replication, and "objective" criteria, tools that are generally inappropriate for the study of paranormal energies and dimensions. Maybe unseen realities are unavailable to scientific inquiry because science exists in time-space, and so-called "paranormal events" exist outside of time-space, and thus have nothing to do with science's time-space laws.

Possibly *efforts to apply the requirements of science to "prove" paranormal events—or to disprove them—will always result in defeat*, because psychic events are no more scientific than a beautiful painting or a great piece of music or a wonderful novel. Yet statistics show consistently that people prayed for do better than those not prayed for, *whether they know they are being prayed for or not!*

My own gradual belief has come, slowly, from looking back with opened eyes and realizing, for instance, that I've always communed with my animals, as well as with dolphins at the Dolphin Research Center on my two week-long forays there, and that I have had dreams that seem beyond coincidence. I have photographed mysterious orbs (and they are not dew drops on my lens!). I have come to believe from synchronicities I have experienced, especially in the last several years. Most of these are in the next book.

My belief comes too from my *reinterpretation* of earlier events in my life, like the ghost of Anna Marie. And of course, I am further persuaded by the stories I've been told by earnest people who have no reason to lie. It doesn't make sense that all, or any, of these people whose reputations are now on the line as much as mine, would lie. And they have all allowed me to use their names.

Imagination is obviously the vehicle for psychic knowings, just as imagination is the vehicle by which we learn scientific information. Imagination ought not to be denigrated. I've had to learn to overcome my own "Oh, it's just my imagination …"

From proven results of the Remote Viewing courses I've taken, it is evident to me now that *mind is not limited to our bodies, but is also non-local,* and can perceive realities at a distance—or perhaps it is not at a distance at all—but other realities co-existent with our own. If I can "go" to a target while in a meditative state, scribble down impressions and even a drawing in the dark with a pencil on a sheet of paper, that matches a target photograph in a sealed envelope, that's enough to assure me that some part of my mind—not my brain, as it stays in my skull—*can leave my body and go somewhere else, observe and return with accurate information.* I have done that not once, but many times.

Visits into the past, reported by many with convincing and provable detail—see for instance *One White Crow* by George McMullen, and *The Search for Omm Sety* by Jonathan Cott—indicate that *something of us is not time-bound.* Our bodies are bound by time and space, but not our minds, not our spirits.

Carrying these indisputable *facts* to their logical conclusion, I now feel certain that when we die to earthly life, some part of our mind or spirit goes on to the next world, or level, or vibration. I expect to do that at death.

The sheer incidence of synchronicity and of lost objects finding their ways back to their owners against all odds ("Oh, that was just a coincidence!") seems evidence that *there is an underlying law or principle guiding events that we just haven't discovered yet.* But quantum physics has already declared that any two particles that have once been in contact retain an attraction to each other forever.

Looking back in my life, I see that I have often learned about things just before I needed them. Perhaps the most startling example of that is how, just before my daughter was born with cerebral palsy and retardation, I had occasion to research parents' reactions to learning that their child is not "perfect." I know that can be seen as a coincidence, but I think it was synchronicity.

We know that psychic phenomena are reported world-wide and have been as long as mankind has been reporting. No culture is, or ever has been, without them. The immanence of the accounts is, I think, another reasonable argument for their being real, and perhaps a better argument than trying to enlist science in their support. The weight of evidence all by itself supports at least some of the things people experience being real. People who reveal their paranormal experiences risk their reputations, their credibility, and their privacy. Though critics argue that people invent psychic phenomena for publicity or self-aggrandizement, many people reporting phenomena are horrified and distressed by them. And some won't even *let* you print them with their names.

But if the jury is still out on most of the phenomena that this book is concerned with, consider this truth: In the *absence of knowing, anything is possible*. Think of the attitudes of Europeans before the exploration of the Americas: because so little was known about the underlying principles of modern science or about the great uncharted western hemisphere, *anything was possible*, including cities of pure gold, fountains of youth, corn that grew "four foot a day" (from the Norwegian folk song "Oleanna"), ring snakes that got around by rolling with their tails held in their mouths, and *wak-wak* trees, whose fruits were fresh young virgins ripe for the picking.

If it seems we are today beyond such folly, I think not. We do not know why some people get cancer and others don't. What's the story? Everyone's got an opinion, but we don't know. Take this supplement, someone tells us. Drink only unchlorinated water. Eat bluegreen algae. Overdose on Vitamin C. Don't live near high tension wires. Eat almonds. Don't eat eggs. Do eat eggs. Laugh a lot.

Drink red wine. Don't drink any alcohol. Drink coffee. No, drink tea. Take estrogen and progesterone. Don't take those dangerous hormones. Don't drink the water; it has mercury, e-coli, and God knows what else in it. Do drink lots of water for its minerals, and trace elements. And still, sometimes the most meticulous people get cancer. And that old man out in that cabin who smokes two packs a day and downs a quart of moonshine every day of his life, and hates vegetables, lives on and on, chuckling at the rest of us fools.

If we don't believe paranormal events are even possible, we won't interpret any events as paranormal. I now think *we are all psychic, and must some day come to acknowledge our potential and gifts.*

As humans I think we are still young in evolution; as proof I offer that most humans are quite like teenagers their whole lives; we thoughtlessly abuse our bodies and our planet; we are governed by our hormones; we are selfish and self-serving; we don't think about the future; and we don't believe we will die.

Having considered the stories in this book and many, many more over the years, I now believe *that at least humans and animals have souls; that we live temporarily in a material world but are citizens of a much greater reality* which, for all our advanced science, is still largely unknowable except through human—and animal—perception.

We have for the last three and a half centuries given power to the material universe and taken power away from the realm of spirit. Perhaps psychic events are merely proof of spirit leaking through. We cannot be fully human, I suspect, until we own, take charge of, and embrace spirit once again. And the weight of evidence, should we choose to look at it squarely, can lead us into belief that will finally allow us see this truth.

17

Further Reading for Spirit Chasers

I will *begin* reading just about *any* book on a paranormal subject, but I quickly abandon those that are self-serving, badly written, paranoid, objectionably pedantic, or, as often occurs, strike me as just plain loony. I much prefer to read books by people who have been scientifically trained to observe dispassionately, people with PhDs and MDs following their names, people associated with respectable universities. Thus I have chosen to read Dr. Ian Stevenson on reincarnation, Dr. Raymond Moody on near-death experiences, Dr. John Mack on UFO encounters, Dr. Brian Weiss on past lives. All are physicians, all trained to be skeptical, and all arrived late and reluctantly at their inescapable conclusions.

Rational writers surprise readers by slipping in paranormal tales. Walter Edmonds, in his elegant memoir, *Tales My Father Never Told*, tells the story of how, one summer, the milk in his father's dairy soured daily; nothing they could do would stop it. Then an Irish servant girl told them they needed to pour some cream each day into the little creek on the property to feed and placate the "little people living in the stream," who she said were souring the milk. Feeling silly, the family did what the girl told them to do. The milk never soured again.

Derek Tangye, in his delightful memoir *Somewhere A Cat is Waiting*, tells of saying, a few hours after a favorite cat had died, "I will never have another cat, unless a pure black one whose home we can never trace should arrive in the middle of a storm." Three months later, *exactly* that event occurred—and of course the untraceable sodden black kitten became a great favorite in her turn.

Paul Broks, in his fascinating book, *Into the Silent Land, Travels in Neuropsychology*, recounts a midnight encounter with a Christmas tree that was physically present—he got up and smelled and touched it before going back to bed. When he awoke and got up later, it was gone. He returned to bed, awoke in daylight, and the tree was back again, and he found himself paralyzed. He closed his eyes: "The room was still a block of sunlight when I opened them again, but there was no tree." (Broks explains this and other mental events like this as mere brain activity.)

The books listed here are carefully chosen out of a mountain of books on various subjects touched on, with a brief description of their contents. These books are on subjects often regarded as "flaky"—but they are books by unflaky people. They are all well-written. These particular criteria required that I leave out some other fascinating books which may also be in their own ways true and even outstanding.

Allen, Mary. THE ROOMS OF HEAVEN, Knopf, 1999. *A non-believer psychically seeks her dead lover. Beautifully written, a model for any average person seeking to communicate with the dead.*

Beck, Martha. EXPECTING ADAM, 1999. *A woman professor at Harvard, highly skeptical, is bombarded with psychic events while awaiting the birth of a Down Syndrome child.*

Borgia, Anthony. LIFE IN THE WORLD UNSEEN, M.A.P., Midway, Utah, 1993. *A channeled description of life after death by a Christian clergyman who, after his death, dictated corrections to all he had written during his life.*

Chopra, Deepak, M.D. QUANTUM HEALING, Bantam, 1987. *America's current most popular proponent of mind-body health. Chopra is an Indian-American physician trained in eastern ayurvedic medicine and western medicine.*

Cott, Jonathan. SEARCH FOR OMM SETY, Warner Books, 1987. *True story, with scholarly documentation and testimony of eminent Egyptologists, of a British woman, Dorothy Eady, who after a fall as a child was "changed" into an ancient Egyptian.*

Cremo, Michael, and Richard L. Thompson. FORBIDDEN ARCHEOLOGY, Bhaktivedanta Books, 1998. *A critical review of suppressed evidence related to human evolution on earth, and an argument for reinvestigation of outdated scientific paradigms.*

Crichton, Michael. TRAVELS, Ballantine Books, 1990. *Physician and popular novelist (Jurrasic Park, etc.) details his personal journey from rationality to spirituality.*

Dossey, Larry, M.D. HEALING WORDS, Harper Collins, 1993. *A medical doctor investigates the possibility that conscious intent has helpful effects even at a distance, even when the sufferer does not know he is being prayed for.* (see next)

Dossey. MEANING AND MEDICINE, Bantam, 1992. *Carefully controlled studies by the Chief of Staff of Medical City Dallas Hospital prove that prayer hastens healing, that illness has meaning far* beyond the conventional explanations of bacteria or viruses, and that mind, meaning, and illness are connected.

Doyle, A. Conan. THE EDGE OF THE UNKNOWN, Putnam, 1930. *Classic investigation of paranormal events, concluding "That they still lived and still loved was the constant message from the beyond, accompanied by many material proofs."*

Dunne, J.W. AN EXPERIMENT WITH TIME, Faber and Faber, 1927. *A classic that appears to prove the reality of seeing the future, thereby demolishing our concept of time.*

Fowler, Raymond. THE ALLAGASH ABDUCTIONS. Wildflower Press, 1993. *One of the two most convincing abduction accounts.*

Fuller, John G. THE INTERRUPTED JOURNEY, Dell Books, 1966. *The famous first, convincing, account of a couple abducted by aliens in 1963.*

Green, Celia and Charles McCreery. APPARITIONS, Oxford, 1975. *Excellent documentation of English ghost stories, divided by type, by two university researchers.*

Greene, Marilyn. FINDER, Crown, 1988. *Fascinating and impressive account of a combined intuitive/intellectual approach for finding lost persons.*

Huxley, Aldous. THE DOORS OF PERCEPTION, and HEAVEN AND HELL, Penguin, 1963. *Famous essays on altered states of consciousness, discussing some drugs that have been among man's traditional doorways to paranormal experiences.*

James, William. THE VARIETIES OF RELIGIOUS EXPERIENCE, Penguin, 1982. *First published in 1902. Has among other discussions the classic one on types of mysticism.*

Liverziano, Filippo. LIFE, DEATH, AND CONSCIOUSNESS, Prism, 1991. *Investigating these three things, he concludes that those who have visited the beyond universally experience difficulty in expressing the experience in human language, a sense of peace, an abandonment of the physical body, and autoscopic experiences.*

Mack, John E., M.D. ABDUCTION, Ballantine, 1994. *This Harvard professor and psychiatrist has risked his reputation reporting on his clients who claim to be abductees by UFOs. Fascinating, terrifying, and sad accounts.*

Mack. PASSPORT TO THE COSMOS, Crown, 1999. *This book studies the meaning of the alien abduction experience. "Crossover of the unseen world into the material world is a regular occurrence in indigenous cultures." Mack argues that something real is going on.*

Mackenzie, Andrew. HAUNTINGS AND APPARITIONS, Granada Publishing, 1983. *Report of carefully investigated hauntings by the British Society of Psychical Research.*

Mackenzie. ADVENTURES IN TIME, Athlone, 1997. *Reports by people who have found themselves suddenly in another time and place. Carefully researched, proof of Haldane's statement, "The world is not only queerer than anyone has imagined but queerer than anyone can imagine." MacKenzie states, "The task of the psychical researcher is, as a rule, beset by disappointments as case after case collapses for lack of supporting evidence ...," and goes on to report some that do not collapse.*

McMullen, George. ONE WHITE CROW, Hampton Roads, 1994. *An amazing account of intuitive archaeology done by the author with Canada's leading archaeologist Dr. J. Norman Emerson, who confirms the accuracy of McMullen's intuition time and time again regarding achaeological sites. McMullen was able to psychically view with great accuracy previous sites where archaeological remains were, and lead diggers specifically to important locations—not once, but over and over.*

Monroe, Robert. JOURNEYS OUT OF THE BODY, Doubleday, 1971. *Report of a remarkable man's unbidden out-of-body experiences, and his subsequent adventures while out of the body. His further books are also interesting.*

Moody, Raymond, M.D. COMING BACK, Bantam, 1991. *This physician and psychiatrist is the foremost authority on near-death experiences by patients brought back from death by state-of-the-art technology. He held a post at the University of Virginia Hospital in Charlottesville for many years, and now lives and practices in Georgia.*

Moody. LIFE AFTER LIFE, Mockingbird Books, 1975. *The first, and still classic, best-seller on near-death experiences.*

Osis, Karlis, Ph.D. and Erlendur Haraldsson, Ph.D. AT THE HOUR OF DEATH, Hastings House, 1997. *Careful treatment of the near-death experience.*

Rico, Gabriele Lusser. WRITING THE NATURAL WAY, Tarcher, 1983. *An effective method for opening creative channels for writing or problem-solving by a simple technique called clustering.*

Ring, Kenneth, Ph.D. HEADING TOWARD OMEGA, Morrow, 1989. *A discussion of the meaning of the near-death experience.*

Ritchie, George G. Jr., M.D., PhD. RETURN FROM TOMORROW, Chosen Books Publishing, 1978. *A near-death experience in 1943 changed this highly-regarded psychiatrist's life forever. This story was the inspiration for Dr. Raymond Moody's work.*

Rogo, D. Scott. THE INFINITE BOUNDARY. Dodd, Mead & Company, 1987. *Can modern mental illness be the result of spirit possession? Can spirits of the dead influence the living? A discussion of the possibility of spirit possession in modern madness.*

Rohr, Richard. DISCOVERING THE ENNEAGRAM, Crossroad, 1992. *An ancient and remarkable Sufi method of understanding human personality—both the self and others.*

Russell, Peter. FROM SCIENCE TO GOD. *The famous author of* THE GLOBAL BRAIN, WHITE HOLE IN TIME, *and* THE TM TECHNIQUE, *details his journey from being a "convinced atheist" to a convinced believer in God.*

Sabom, Michael. RECOLLECTIONS OF DEATH, Harper and Row, 1982. *A rational physician investigates the near-death experience.*

Scott, Cyril, Editor. THE BOY WHO SAW TRUE, C. W. Daniel Co., Ltd, Essex, England, 1953. *A convincing and supposedly true Victorian diary (edited by Cyril Scott and in print ever since) by a psychic child, who didn't understand that the rest of the world was not. I have no way to judge its truthfulness, but it's a wonderful book to read.*

Sheldrake, Rupert. SEVEN EXPERIMENTS THAT COULD CHANGE THE WORLD, Riverhead Books, 1995. *How does your pet know you are coming home? Can people tell when they're being stared at from behind? How do termites build two towers that meet exactly in the middle? And more. An invitation to explore the unknown and create new science.*

Shroder, Tom. OLD SOULS. Simon and Schuster, 1999. *A skeptical journalist is made a believer as he follows Ian Stevenson on his investigations of children who remember past lives.*

Siegel, Bernie, M.D. LOVE, MEDICINE, & MIRACLES, Harper and Row, 1986. *A classic about how to be pro-active in self-healing.*

Snow, Robert. LOOKING FOR CARROLL BECKWITH, Daybreak Books, 1999. *An astonishing document by a skeptical police captain who found a past life he had lived or somehow remembered.*

Stevenson, Ian, M.D. TWENTY CASES SUGGESTIVE OF REINCARNATION, University Press of Virginia, 1974. *Stevenson is a physician, a psychiatrist, an excruciatingly painstaking researcher who has become the world authority on reincarnation. He still holds an honored post at U. Va. in Charlottesville.*

Stevenson. CHILDREN WHO REMEMBER PREVIOUS LIVES, University Press of Virginia, 1987. *The weight of evidence is strong in this book.*

Sylvia, Claire. A CHANGE OF HEART, Warner Books, 1997. *A woman who receives a donor heart communicates with the previous owner of the heart. The book details other examples of this new phenomenon.*

Vallee, Jacques. PASSPORT TO MAGONIA, Contemporary Books, 1969. *An account by a world authority of 100 years of UFO sightings worldwide, and a persuasive argument that fairy tales, monster stories, elves and gnomes, represent ancient human encounters with alien entities.*

Wakefield, Dan. EXPECT A MIRACLE, Harper Collins, 1995. *An account by a skeptical writer of the "miracles" that occur to ordinary people. Interesting, as it sensitizes us to the fact that extraordinary things occur often in the ordinary world.*

Watson, Lyall. THE SECRET LIFE OF INANIMATE OBJECTS, Destiny Books, 1992. *Thousands of documented anecdotes of the strange behavior of things. The weight of evidence is particularly strong.*

Wickland, Carl, M.D. THIRTY YEARS AMONG THE DEAD, Coles Publishing, 1980. *The classic book from about 1930 detailing a psychiatrist's effort to aid the mentally ill by using his wife as a channel. His conclusion: that mentally ill patients are suffering from soul-possession by people who are dead and unaware or resentful of having passed out of life.*

Zaleski, Carol. OTHERWORLD JOURNEYS, Oxford, 1987. *Historical examination of near-death and other out-of-body experiences over 500 years, by a Harvard professor.*

Zukav, Gary. THE SEAT OF THE SOUL, Simon and Schuster, 1989. *Premise: man is evolving from a five-sense animal to a multisense animal. "...just as there came a time when the use of candles became inappropriate because of the discovery of electricity," a Newtonian view of the world is no longer tenable in light of what mankind is learning from quantum physics.*

Touches of the paranormal occur without apology in more and more modern books: Bill Bryson's A WALK IN THE WOODS, *and John Berendt's* MIDNIGHT IN THE GARDEN OF GOOD AND EVIL *are two best-sellers that come to mind immediately.*

Sylvia Fraser's THE FOURTH MONKEY, *Walter Edmond's* TALES MY FATHER NEVER TOLD, *Derek Tangye's* SOMEWHERE A CAT IS WAITING, *Paul Broks'* INTO THE SILENT LAND, *my own* WHEN THE FIGHTING IS ALL OVER, *all contain anecdotes by skeptical people who have experienced remarkable and (rationally) unexplainable events.*

Printed in the United States
77650LV00004B/229-471